D1389404

# LATIN AMERICANS
## HUGH O'SHAUGHNESSY

# LATIN AMERICANS
## HUGH O'SHAUGHNESSY

BBC BOOKS

ACKNOWLEDGEMENTS

I would like to thank those who helped to produce this book
including Gill Coleridge, the staff of BBC Books
and, very particularly, Mick Webb, the producer of the Radio 4 series,
who taught me something about making programmes.
My thanks, too, to my son Luke for his work on the index

Grateful acknowledgement is also due to the following
for permission to reprint extracts in this book:

Eduardo Crawley for *Dictators never die*;
Macmillan Publishers Ltd
for *Peru 1870–1977: growth and policy in an open economy*
by Rosemary Thorp and Geoffrey Bertram;
Macmillan Publishing Co. Inc., New York,
for *Latin America: a general history* by John Edwin Fagg;
John Lynch for *The Spanish American revolutions, 1808–1826*.

Published by BBC Books,
a division of BBC Enterprises Limited
Woodlands, 80 Wood Lane, London W12 0TT
First published 1988
© Hugh O'Shaughnessy, 1988
ISBN 0 563 21373 6

Set 11/13 in Palatino by Phoenix Photosetting, Chatham
Printed and bound in Great Britain by Mackays of Chatham Limited

For Fiona and Isobel
from a godfather who has too often forgotten
their birthdays

# CONTENTS

———

# LIST OFILLUSTRATIONS

---

# JULIO ETCHART

———

The black and white photographs on pages 65–80 were taken by Julio Etchart. Etchart was born in Montevideo, Uruguay, in 1950, and trained in photography and 16mm film-making at the University of Montevideo. He came to Europe in 1973, following the military coup in Uruguay, and settled in Britain in 1975, working as a photographer, interpreter and translator.

Etchart has travelled extensively in Latin America, Europe, North Africa and the Middle East, covering a variety of social and political topics. His work has been published in many leading newspapers and magazines, including *The Times*, *The Observer*, *The Economist*, *Time*, *Newsweek*, *Der Spiegel*, *Stern* and *El Pais*. He has also worked for a number of international aid agencies and human rights groups such as Oxfam, War on Want, CAFOD, Amnesty International, the Chile Solidarity Campaign and Committee for Human Rights and the Nicaragua Solidarity Campaign.

# AUTHOR'S NOTE

———

Without descending into pedantry, it might be useful here to define terms. Latin America is a political and cultural term. South, Central and North America are geographical terms. 'Latin America' defines that part of the western hemisphere which was colonised and remained under the influence of the three Latin countries of Europe. Haïti was occupied by the French, Brazil by the Portuguese and all the rest of Latin America by the Spanish. Latin America therefore extends through South America to Central America and to that part of North America occupied by Mexico. All South Americans – with the exception of the inhabitants of the former British and Dutch colonies of Guyana and Surinam – are Latin Americans, but not all Latin Americans are South Americans. Mexicans are clearly Latin Americans but not South Americans. The West Indians are sometimes considered Latin Americans and sometimes not.

Latin Americans object to United States citizens appropriating to themselves the term 'Americans': there are, after all, more Latin than US Americans, more of America is Latin than Anglo-Saxon and the Latins got there first. Latin Americans normally call US citizens *norteamericanos* or 'North Americans' – although that Latin American usage ignores the Canadians and overlooks the fact that most of Mexico is geographically in North America. The French Canadians do not think of themselves, and are not thought of, as Latin Americans, though they speak a Latin language and clearly live in America.

# RECENT CHRONOLOGY

**1946**  *February*  Juan Domingo Perón elected President of Argentina.

**1949**  *November*  Costa Rica abolishes army.

**1952**  *April*  President Víctor Paz Estenssoro starts major social revolution in Bolivia and disbands army.

**1954**  *May*  General Alfredo Stroessner seizes power in Paraguay.
*June*  Elected civilian government of Guatemala overthrown by right-wing officers with US assistance.

**1955**  Perón overthrown by military coup.

**1959**  *January*  Fidel Castro enters Havana in triumph.

**1961**  *April*  Bay of Pigs invasion of Cuba.
*May*  President Rafael Trujillo of the Dominican Republic, dictator since 1947, assassinated.

**1962**  *October*  Cuban missile crisis.
*November*  President Paz of Bolivia overthrown by re-formed army.
Mario Vargas Llosa publishes *La Ciudad y los Perros* ('The Time of the Hero').

**1964**  *April*  Military seize power in Brazil.
Eduardo Frei elected president of Chile in sweeping 'earthquake' victory.

**1965**  *April*  US Marines invade Dominican Republic.
*May*  Inter-American Peace Force of the Organisation of American States formed in the Dominican Republic.

**1966**  *June*  Military overthrow civilian President Illia in Argentina.

**1967**  *October*  Ernesto 'Ché' Guevara shot after capture by Bolivian army.

**1968**  Medellín conference of Latin American bishops.
*October*  General Juan Velasco seizes power in Peru.

**1969** Four-day 'football war' between El Salvador and Honduras.

**1970** *December* Dr Salvador Allende, a Socialist heading left-wing Popular Unity coalition, becomes president of Chile.

**1973** *June* Perón returns to Argentina and is later re-elected president.
*September* General Augusto Pinochet seizes power in Chile.

**1974** *July* Perón dies in office in Buenos Aires aged 78.

**1976** *January* Venezuela nationalises foreign oil companies.
*March* General Jorge Videla topples President María Estela de Perón, Perón's third wife and successor.

**1979** Puebla meeting of Latin American bishops.
*July* Victory for popular insurrection in Nicaragua led by Sandinistas against the Somoza dynasty.
*October* General Carlos Humberto Romero ousted in El Salvador by reformist coup.
*October* US-controlled Canal Zone in Panama abolished by bilateral agreement. Panamanians participate in the administration of the Canal.

**1980** *March* Archbishop Oscar Romero of San Salvador murdered.

**1982** *April* Argentine invasion of the Falkland Islands.
*June* British recapture of Port Stanley.

**1983** *October* US invasion of Grenada.

**1984** *September* Foreign ministers of the European Community meet their Central American counterparts in San José.

**1985** *April* José Sarney becomes first civilian president of Brazil since 1964.

**1986** *June* Jorge Luis Borges dies.

**1987** *August* Five Central American presidents meeting in Guatemala agree on joint peace plan.

# PREFACE
# OF AN ENTHUSIAST

---

'How long has Hugh been writing about Latin America now?' said the man from *The Times* to a friend of mine at a cocktail party.

'It must be about twenty-five years,' she replied.

'That's much too long, much too long. He should have gone on to something else a long time ago.'

The trouble is that I haven't often wanted to go on to anything else. The job of trying to describe and interpret Latin America to Europeans seems to me a reasonable enough vocation, I enjoy it and it earns me a living wage.

On second thoughts – and, I hope, without sounding pompous or self-absorbed – I should have expressed those sentiments much more forcefully. The job is an important one, given the misconceptions that have spontaneously grown up and the falsities which have deliberately been coined about the region. The opportunity to travel and learn about the most beautiful, complex, diverse and interesting part of the world outside of Europe itself is as enthralling a one as any journalist could wish for.

The region is one of enormous geographical diversity. Flying south from Santiago to Punta Arenas, I have seen the glaciers creep off the lowest slopes of the Andes into the sea and freeze the waters for miles around them. In Costa Rica I have trudged through the lava up the side of an active volcano and eased my feet by bathing them in the hot waters of the stream flowing from the summit.

In Port of Spain – to include the West Indies in Latin America for a moment – I have driven in a tropical downpour so intense that it was not possible to see the front edge of the bonnet of the Land Rover. In Peru there are textiles from before the time of Columbus, every stitch of which has been perfectly preserved over the centuries in a dry desert atmosphere where rain is unknown.

In Grenada there is cinnamon to be cut from the bark of a delicate tropical tree; in the forests of Panama, the lemon-flavoured sap which surrounds the beans in a freshly plucked cocoa pod is there to be enjoyed. In Peru, stews of potatoes of a flavour and succulence long ago lost by the potatoes which were brought to Europe are there to nourish the traveller in the high Andes. I have met a flock of llamas on the road in Bolivia, chased vainly after an armadillo in Venezuela and watched the sacred jaguars in Belize.

Throughout the region, man for thousands of years has battled to tame, harness and improve on nature in a way which makes human effort in many other parts of the world seem almost paltry. Surely there can be no more spectacular site for a human settlement of ancient days than Machu Picchu, built on top of a mountain in Peru and commanding a magnificent panorama of the jungle. If there is one, it is to be found at Palenque where, on a mountain site also overlooking the jungle, the Incas' mastery of the art of hewing and forming blocks of stone weighing hundreds of tons gives way to the Mayas' grace and delicacy with brick and mortar. The Mayas achieved it all without recourse to metal or to the use of the wheel.

The excitement of standing at Machu Picchu or Palenque, in the Mayan ceremonial centre of Uxmal or in the Inca fortress of Sacsahuamán, is compounded by the realisation that there must be scores of lost cities waiting to be found by the knowledgeable and adventurous, cities whose remains will shed light on the still shadowy histories of the peoples who inhabited America before the Europeans arrived.

When I first went to Latin America I understood how Columbus could have reported back to Spain that he had found the terrestrial paradise complete with the four rivers of Genesis which proceeded from the Tree of Life. It was so rich, he said, that with its resources he could raise an army of 100 000 foot soldiers and 10 000 cavalrymen.

I also understood a little of what the old soldier Bernal Díaz del Castillo, a member of Hernán Cortés' expedition against the Aztecs in 1519, felt when they got to their destination.

During the morning we arrived at a broad causeway and continued our march towards Iztapalapa, and when we

saw so many cities and villages built in the water and other
great towns on dry land and that straight and level causeway
going towards Mexico, we were amazed and said that it was
like the enchantments they tell of in the legend of Amadis,
on account of the great towers and temples and buildings
rising from the water, and all built of masonry. And some
of our soldiers even asked whether the things that we saw
were not a dream.

In various spots of Latin America the mute stones tell more elo-
quently than any chronicle of the tragic and murderous clash of
culture which occurred in the sixteenth century when the
European took command over the native. At the village of Mitla in
the southern Mexican state of Oaxaca, for instance, the Christian
conquerors built a graceful church with baroque cupolas, such as
you can see in any south European town, on top of ancient temples
whose stone friezes bear witness to the delicate aesthetic sense of
the races they conquered. In Cuzco, the Inca capital, the Dominican church of Santo Domingo sits on what used to be the Incas'
temple of the sun.

While it would be wrong to romanticise the circumstances in
which greedy and triumphant Europeans landed on and seized the
New World, the juxtaposition of familiar and exotic cultures which
'the Discovery of America' brought about has, for me, been at the
centre of Latin America's fascination.

The ability to roam the region and communicate almost everywhere in one or other of two European languages; to recognise the
transplanted architectural styles of the Old World; to discern the
historical influence of the Spanish Inquisition or the Portuguese
monarchy, the French Revolution or England's Industrial Revolution, cannot but be thrilling for someone brought up in Europe.

But the direct influence of Europe is transformed and enriched in
Latin America by the Europeans' encounter with other races.
Though badly mauled by Spanish and Portuguese conquerors, the
native civilisations have subsisted and are finally becoming more
assertive of their personalities and their rights. There are, too, the
black populations – in many countries, slaves were imported from
Africa to do the labouring which the Europeans were too few and
too proud to undertake and which the indigenous people were too
weakened to keep up. And this encounter takes place where there
is a fast-growing population living in space that is generally

17

unused and among natural resources that are still unexploited. How much food could not be produced if the Latin Americans put to use that three-quarters of the continent's potentially useful land which the agronomists say is lying idle? How much oil could not be found in the region if as many wells were drilled per square kilometre as there have been in the United States? How many precious minerals will be found when the soil of Latin America has been as thoroughly prospected as Britain's has since the Iron Age? How much power would there not be if the region's rivers were dammed? For cultural and material reasons, then, Latin American societies, for all their many injustices and rigidities, are still in the making, still not set in the rigid cultural moulds of European – or indeed Muslim, Hindu or Japanese – societies. The struggle of new societies to emerge meanwhile gives the journalist an enormous wealth of subjects to write about and, if he or she is lucky, events to witness, from day to day.

Running through Latin American societies, moreover, are two contradictory sentiments. The first is the feeling that Latin America is still what it was in the sixteenth century, an Eldorado where enjoyment of the good life need not necessarily mean great personal effort. The feeling is that the region is blessed by nature with fertile land, seas teeming with fish and the earth bursting with valuable minerals of all kinds. For me this feeling was almost tangible in Venezuela on my first visit to Latin America in the early 1960s. Well before the big jump in oil prices in 1973, the Venezuelans enjoyed an enviable life as petroleum exporters. Foreigners, whom they did not have to pay but who paid them, came to pump out of the ground limitless quantities of oil which the Venezuelans had just inherited. The Venezuelans had no other worry than to make sure the foreigners were paying what seemed a reasonable price for the privilege of working in Venezuela. The income was assured, the climate pleasant, tropical fruit fell from the trees and the money in the streets was coined out of pure silver. The more menial tasks such as building the skyscrapers, sweeping the streets, cooking the food and minding the children, were performed by millions of men and women who had immigrated from neighbouring Colombia. Venezuela was only the most recent of a series of Eldorados. Mexico and Peru had been Eldorados when silver was discovered there, Chile was an Eldorado during the nitrate boom, Argentina and Uruguay were Eldorados when the world demanded the meat, cereals and wool they could turn out in vast quantities.

Governing the inhabitants of these Eldorados, on the other hand, is a nightmare which only the boldest and most ambitious want to live through. Simon Bolivar, the man who liberated northern South America from Spanish colonial rule and had more experience of the former subjects of imperial Spain in the first years of independence than anyone, gloomily summed up the lessons of a lifetime in a letter he wrote from Barranquilla in Colombia a month before his death in 1830.

'I have arrived at only a few sure conclusions:
1   For us, America is ungovernable.
2   He who serves a revolution ploughs the sea.
3   The only thing we can do in America is to emigrate.
4   This country will eventually fall into the hands of the unbridled mob, and will proceed to almost imperceptible petty tyrannies of all complexions and races.
5   Devoured as we are by every kind of crime and annihilated by ferocity, Europeans will not go to the trouble of conquering us.
6   If it were possible for any part of the world to revert to primordial chaos, that would be America's final state.'

The chapters which follow are no more than snapshots, or better, composite pictures of various groups of Latin Americans. They were all taken and assembled with the help of Latin Americans themselves whose friendship I have enjoyed or whose anger I have provoked. The help I have received from Latin Americans of all sorts and the special camaraderie I have experienced from journalists in the region have never ceased to amaze me. Even the disagreeable moments I have undergone in the region have proved useful. When the Pinochet dictatorship expelled me from Chile twice in the early 1980s I took it as a compliment. Here, at least, was proof that one's words were read and taken seriously.

Latin America has also provided me with a political education of a thoroughness and forcefulness which I would never have found had I limited my interests to Britain and the rest of Europe. Having seen the conditions in which so many tens of millions of Latin Americans live, I shall never again fall for the argument that what Latin America wants now is a period of 'stability'. It will certainly want a period of stability in the future. But first the Pinochets and the Stroessners have to be swept away and much more real democracy given to those who, like the Salvadoreans and the Guatemalans, are able to vote but not to bring about a change in their lives.

The people of the region are no better and no worse than the rest of us. At times they can bear out the worst despairing fears of Bolivar. Like Europeans, they can sink to the depths of barbarity and treachery but, like any other set of people, they can also muddle along in mediocrity and rise to heights of achievement and heroism. The chapters which follow aim to make them better understood. I would recommend those who can do so to travel to Latin America to check on the veracity of my opinions. They will almost certainly enjoy the experience: they will undoubtedly learn much more than they expected.

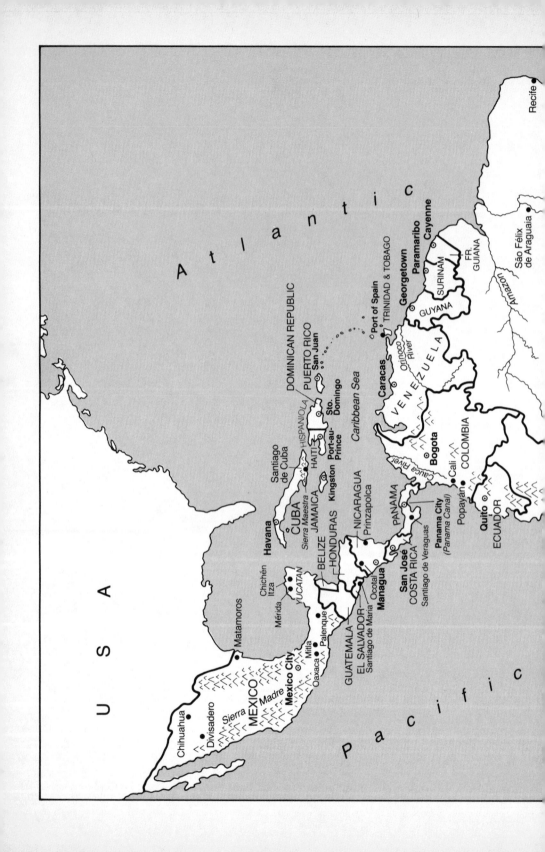

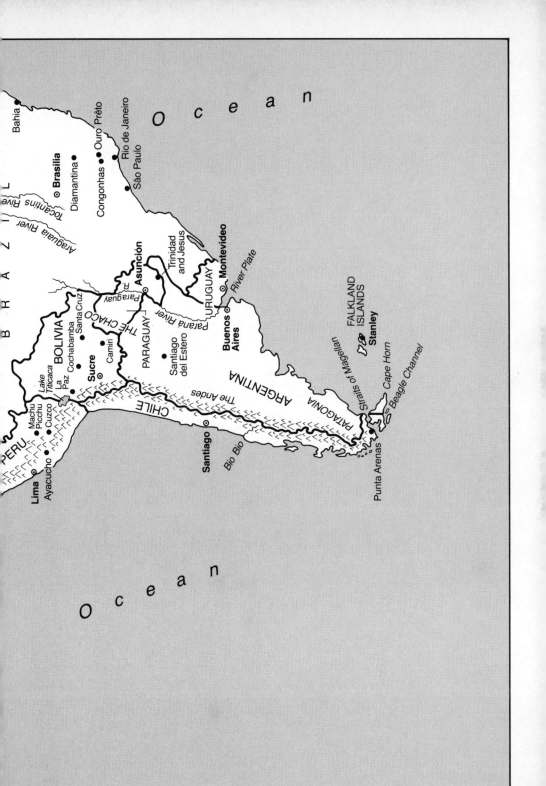

# CHAPTER ONE

# WHO ARE THEY?

*We are neither Europeans nor Indians but a mixed species midway between aborigines and Spaniards . . .*
*Thus our position is most extraordinary and complicated.*

SIMON BOLIVAR

*Our country – our countries – are in a deep sense more a fiction than a reality.*

MARIO VARGAS LLOSA

━━━

The situation of the Latin Americans has become a great deal more extraordinary and more complicated since Bolivar wrote the above words in 1826. Having liberated what are today the republics of Venezuela, Colombia, Panama and Ecuador – the whole of northern South America – from the colonial rule of the Spaniards, the brilliant Venezuelan general had hopes of welding all the former colonies of Spain into one nation. (Brazil, which was to become the largest of the countries of Latin America, still belonged to Portugal.)

'The great day of America has not yet dawned,' an exultant Bolivar said. 'We have expelled our [Spanish] oppressors, broken the tablets of their tyrannical laws and founded legitimate institutions. But we still need to establish the basis of the social compact, which ought to form of this world a nation of republics.'

That was not to be. Stretching from northern California to Cape Horn, the vast land mass which had been miraculously kept together politically by civil servants in Spain and Spanish viceroys and soldiers on the spot broke into pieces once the authority of the Bourbons was taken away. The Latin American states divided and subdivided like amoebas. Bolivar's Gran Colombia split into three; Venezuela, Colombia and Ecuador. The Central Americans stuck together precariously for a decade or two before breaking into five different republics; Guatemala, Honduras, El Salvador, Nicaragua and Costa Rica. The Spaniards themselves hung on grimly against increasing local resistance in Cuba and Puerto Rico till the US finally completed the job started by the Cuban insurgents and chased them away ignominiously in 1898. The last Latin American republic emerged only in this century when, in 1903, Panama split off from Colombia and, with Washington's backing, declared itself independent.

There could have been even greater fission in the bigger states such as Argentina had not strong men of vision held their countries together by the force of their characters and their arms. To this day big swathes of land in the provinces give only the most grudging allegiance to the governments in the national capitals. In Bolivia the eastern lowland city of Santa Cruz, rich with the cocaine trade and oil, sees little reason to obey the president in La Paz, where the tin mines are exhausted and the peasants scratch a painful living high up in the Andes where there is little vegetation. As late as the beginning of the Second World War, the two cities were linked only by mule train and a faltering airline. In Mexico, Yucatán, sticking out into the Caribbean Sea and reached from Mexico City after two nights in the train or by car via four ferries, remembers its bid for independence last century. In Ecuador the people of the stiflingly hot tropical banana port of Guayaquil on the Pacific disdain the dreamers of Quito, the cool and rainy capital 3000 metres up in the Andes. Even in comparatively small Nicaragua the ill feeling between the conservative city of Granada and the liberal city of León was such that Managua had to be declared the compromise capital in the middle of the nineteenth century.

Meanwhile Brazil stood aloof from the rest. Vast, self-sufficient in many ways, Portuguese-speaking and with different traditions from the Spanish speakers, Brazil was first dependent on the Portuguese crown, then for nearly seventy years an empire with an emperor of its own and, from 1889 onwards, a republic. Prospering with investments made by British entrepreneurs, the Brazilians saw little need to have much to do with their Spanish-speaking neighbours. They have not changed their attitudes very much to this day.

Divided one from another by enormous deserts and high mountains, the independent republics would have been hard put to it to achieve unity even had they ever wanted to. But in every republic local governments were installed and few were willing to surrender their powers, once established, to others. Each area had displayed its own distinctive characteristics in colonial times – some had many native peoples, some none; some had big black slave populations, in some slavery was virtually unknown; some, like the seats of the viceroyalties, had printing presses and pretensions to refinement and education, others were cultural deserts. After independence, with the Spanish crown no longer a focus of loyalty, these differences were solidified. The new republics grew apart.

The biggest Latin American country in area, population and resources of all sorts is Brazil with 140 million people, a poor country but still one of the largest economies in the world. The most populous country of Spanish America is Mexico with 80 million. The dwarf is Panama with a little over 2 million. But the differences are not just between the big and the small. In Venezuela, Uruguay and Argentina more than four people out of five live in cities. The Venezuelans live in Caracas and Maracaibo and don't really worry about the countryside. So blasé are they about the oil money that the majority feel agriculture is beneath them: why should they worry about tilling the land when they can employ immigrant Colombians to plough, sow and harvest? Why worry even about the Colombians when they can phone up and have food flown in from Miami? In Argentina and Uruguay agriculture is the backbone of the economy but it survives in a fashion which would be thought wasteful and primitive in Britain, France or the Netherlands.

In Haïti, on the other hand, more than seven out of ten people still live in the countryside. Before the slaves rose up and massacred their masters in 1791, Haïti (or Saint-Domingue as it was known) was a French colony whose sugar produced staggering wealth and whose white population was cultured enough to stage concerts and produce operas, some of which they wrote themselves. Now the estates are gone, the forests have been cut down for firewood, the land is exhausted and eroded and the average income no more than about £4 a week for every man, woman and child. Virtually every Argentine and Uruguayan can read and write but more than three out of five Haïtians cannot.

While a big majority of the inhabitants of Guatemala and Bolivia are descended from pre-Colombian indigenes, there are few black or brown faces in neighbouring Costa Rica and Argentina. Under the constitution which was in force in Costa Rica until 1948, blacks were even forbidden to live anywhere but on the Caribbean coast. Nor, of course, are the indigenes themselves one undifferentiated group of people. In Mexico alone there are an estimated 17 million Indians split into 56 groups or nations, each speaking its own language. The variegated mixes of blood between the races, from pure white through brown and yellow to black, are the basis of much social posturing. In the Creole language of Haïti, there are said to be 107 words for the different colours of the skin and variety of features. In his book *The Latin Americans*, the Mexican writer Víctor Alba quotes a satirical epitaph from Peru:

> Here lies Manongo
> Of pure Latin race:
> His mother came from China,
> His grandfather from the Congo.

The racialism which sprung up because of those differences, though never as strong as the racialism left behind in many parts of their empire by the British, has reinforced the divisions between rich and poor for which the region has become notorious. There has been an unwillingness on the part of the richest and most powerful people in most Latin American countries to countenance the sort of social changes which gave the United States and Western Europe, Canada and Australasia a prosperous and numerous middle class. As a consequence, most of the republics have a small Europeanised or cosmopolitan élite who are in general richer than their counterparts in the developed world. Their precarious fortunes depend on the efforts of the poor majority. As a further consequence, most Latin American countries have not been able to develop those mass markets for industrial goods which founded the fortunes of the richer countries of the world. It is interesting to note that, according to calculations by the United Nations Economic Commission for Latin America, the share of national income going to the poorest in Latin America is often more or less the same as that in the developed world. The difference between Latin America on the one hand and western European countries and the United States on the other is that the richest five per cent in these countries have twice or three times the share of national wealth that the richest five per cent of European or US citizens enjoy. Brazil and El Salvador are particularly glaring examples of that fact.

In San Salvador and Guatemala City, Rio de Janeiro or Bogota for instance, poverty and riches are squashed close up together. In the richest parts of the city among the skyscrapers and the luxury hotels, colonies of the poorest people live in shacks tucked into the ravines or up on the hillsides. With the rains they are in mortal danger of having their dwellings swept away by the floodwaters.

Some cities seem to be nothing but slum. I well remember a bus journey in El Salvador in the early 1960s long before the present civil war broke out. As we pulled into the bus station of the town of Santa Ana, the beggars, children and old people who were gathering round, and the general filth of the place, made me think I had been transported to some lower ring of Dante's Inferno.

The contrast is quite as great, but not so obvious, in the new capital of Brasília. Since it became the Brazilian capital in 1960, the city has grown to nearly 1 500 000 people. The centre had been planned by Lúcio Costa and Oscar Niemeyer for people of all incomes. Shaped like a bow and arrow beside an artificial ornamental lake, the centre of Brasília is an airy, spacious place, pagan and futuristic rather than pious and old like the centres of other capitals. But today the demand for living accommodation is such that diplomats are living in flats originally designed for plumbers and carpenters and the carpenters and plumbers have gone off to live elsewhere. At one point as the new capital was being built, the pollution from the workers' shanties was killing everything in the lake. The workers were then tidied away to specially planned suburbs over the hill and out of sight of the inhabitants of the capital. There they live to this day, in severe rows of wooden huts built in straight lines like Soweto. The municipal services the inhabitants receive are minimal.

But people continue to flow from the countryside into the inexorably growing cities. They do so not because they are stupid but because they judge that conditions in the cities, however bad, are superior to those they have left behind. The cities hold opportunities that the land can never offer. Very often a network of relations, friends and acquaintances, who have gone to the cities from the immigrant's own country district, are able to help him or her settle. Schools for children exist in the cities, there are doctors and hospitals, there are jobs. None of these may be easily accessible to a newcomer and his family from the countryside. They may not be accessible at all. But in large parts of the countryside they simply do not exist. In almost all the republics, the average income in the towns is two or three times that of the country.

In only a few countries of Latin America is there a sense of community in society, a sense that the gap between rulers and ruled is not unbridgeable. Costa Rica certainly does have that sense. Uruguay, with a relatively homogenous population and a smaller gap between rich and poor than in many republics, did have it; but then in 1973 the military seized power and started the reign of terror. There is a great deal of community feeling in Cuba but the mode of government, in which one man has made every major administrative decision since 1959 and organised opposition and expression of dissent is forbidden, does not foster the idea of participation in decision-making. The greatest sense of community is probably to be found in Nicaragua. There despite the war-weariness people, especially the young, are drawn together by the shared need to resist foreign aggression and by the fact that more progress has been made towards genuine political pluralism and economic democracy than anywhere else in Central America, except Belize.

As class divisions have remained strong, militating against a sense of community in society, so, over the centuries, national stereotypes have grown up helping to divide one country from the other. The Argentines, for example, the most cultivated, welcoming and friendly of peoples, are seen by their fellow Latin Americans as being overbearing and arrogant. Consequently jokes abound.

'What is an Argentine?'
'An Italian who speaks Spanish and thinks he's English.'

'The Argentine goes on holiday to visit his many relations in Italy and at Rome airport makes straight for the nearest telephone booth.

'"Ché," he says to his wife in amazement, using the particularly Argentine form of endearment, "Look how many Argentine names there are in the telephone directory!"'

With their oil money the Venezuelans, in my experience the most generous of Latin Americans, are seen by fellow Latin Americans as nouveaux riches to a man. The Colombians, with their literary and academic traditions, have the reputation of being prissy. Hondurans and Bolivians are both slow movers. Chileans are wildly nationalistic and warlike. Salvadoreans are hardworking. Mexicans all wear big cowboy hats, shooting first and asking questions afterward. Costa Ricans, 'Ticos', are white and smug. Each nationality has by now its own caricature of itself and of the rest. Divided by geography, customs and ways of life, it would have been miraculous if the countries of the region had not drifted apart from each other.

## Bonds of unity

The process of differentiation has been going on now for more than a century and a half, but at the same time the bonds of unity are still very numerous. The big unifying factor in Latin America, outside Brazil and Haïti, is the language. Spanish spoken in one part of the region can generally be understood in all others. An educated Spanish speaker can read Portuguese and even understand the gist of a conversation in Brazil, and the educated Brazilian has few difficulties in Spanish America. Each can read the other's newspapers and books and understand the other's radio and TV.

Differences in vocabulary, for sure, make for hilarity and embarrassment. The word *guagua* means 'bus' in Cuba and 'baby' in Chile. The very common word *coger*, 'to take', means exclusively to take in a sexual sense in Argentina and leads to laughter in Buenos Aires when Spaniards come and recount how many buses and taxis they have taken.

The Argentine word for 'waiter' is *mozo* ('boy'), and the Chilean is *garzón*, a polite derivation from the French. Great offence is caused in Santiago and the Chilean seaside resort of Viña del Mar when Argentine tourists descend on cafés calling for the *mozo*. The Mexican word for waiter, *joven*, means 'young man' in standard Spanish, yet even the frailest octogenarian serving in any Mexico City restaurant comes to such a call.

The Latin Americans have adopted the Spanish and Portuguese usage with surnames. Spanish Americans tack their mother's maiden name to their father's. Laura, whose father was Juan Pérez and whose mother was Josefina Urriolagoitia, would be Laura

31

Pérez Urriolagoitia. When Laura married Adolfo Ugarte she would become Laura Pérez Urriolagoitia de Ugarte or Laura de Ugarte. The Brazilians, who are even more fascinated by names than the Spanish Americans and who manufacture new Christian names with inexhaustible inventiveness, do things in a different order. Wanderley, whose father was Edilson Schneider and whose mother was Clotilda Tavares, would be Wanderley Tavares Schneider.

In Argentina and Uruguay and parts of Central America, *tú* ('you') is replaced by *vos* (roughly 'thou'). This usage has long since died out in Spain, a fact which gives a special sensation of surprise and friendly intimacy to Spanish-speakers coming from other places.

Whatever the local linguistic idiosyncracies, this sharing of language allows all Latin Americans to communicate with each other and lets all educated Latin Americans enjoy their writers and take a common pride in those who have achieved fame outside the region.

With the two principal common languages goes a sense of common history deriving from the experience of being the colonies of two Iberian powers whose own roots were inextricably intermingled. All of Latin America was colonised by Europeans who spoke similar languages, professed Catholicism, sought glory and profit for their monarchs and for themselves. For more than three centuries from 1492 the original natives were subjugated and the region was administered for the ultimate benefit of the crowns of Spain and Portugal. The ties of empire throughout the region were cut, in most cases by violent means, in the first three decades of the nineteenth century. The weight of shared history is a heavy one.

Religion, as we shall see later, is a link which binds all the Latin American countries together irrespective of differences of language. The Roman Catholic religion arrived with Columbus and with the first Portuguese settlers and has sent down such deep roots that now Brazil is the largest 'Catholic country' and Latin American Catholics outnumber those from any other region of the world.

In religion, as in so many other things, there can be no uniformity in Latin America. The region is not as pious and as churchgoing as, say, Ireland or Poland. Religion in Latin America has never been a refuge for national feeling persecuted by non-

Catholic invaders, a *Volkskirche*, as it was in those two countries. Catholic culture is only skin deep in many countries. In some areas where pre-Colombian cultures are still strong or the blacks have memories of how their African ancestors worshipped, the Catholic cosmogony is mixed up with non-Christian beliefs. In Brazil many people in all strata of society, from beggars to ambassadors, practise spiritism. They appease the old gods with offerings of food and drink and attend seances, reaching out to the dead and to spirit guides and going into ecstatic trances.

In other areas, notably Central America, the influence of well-financed Protestant sects from the United States has grown, bringing conservative political views, the extreme individualism of the 'American dream' and a hostility to the view of society as a community whose members have some sort of responsibility for each other. The Mennonites, those strange, simple but litigious believers whose faith goes back to an early renaissance Dutch divine, have found homes in Latin America, particularly in Paraguay. The Anglicans, a small monument to Britain's missionary urge, maintain some dioceses, especially in southern South America. Even so, religious allegiances in those many places where they exist are principally to the Roman Church. While it would today be rash to presume that any particular Latin American was a Catholic, it would be reasonable to suppose that he or she was familiar with the culture of Catholicism, whether that person accepted it or not.

The internal domestic ties of language, history and religion and perhaps Bolivar's still-surviving dream of making 'a nation of republics' have been strengthened on a political level by the sense of facing common threats from the outside. The United States has very often provided such a threat. In 1823 President James Monroe declared his country's opposition to any further attempts at colonisation in the western hemisphere by the European powers. It did not promise that the United States itself would not seek to expand its influence in the hemisphere. The Monroe Doctrine, as it came to be known, was of little import to the Europeans. They continued to intervene actively in the politics of the region and the young United States was powerless to prevent them. The threat to the Latin Americans implied in the Doctrine first became a reality when the expanding power of the United States, and the ineptitude of Mexico's rulers, allowed Washington to take over a quarter or more of the territory of Mexico, including what are now the US states of California, Texas, New Mexico, Nevada, Oregon and Arizona. Only the Spanish place names remain as a reminder that they were once part of the Spanish empire and of Mexico: San Francisco, Los Angeles, Sacramento, Santa Fe, Las Vegas.

In the succeeding century US soldiers were to come to Mexico again and again, to annex Puerto Rico and to occupy Haïti, the Dominican Republic, Cuba, Panama, Nicaragua for spells. Throughout the Caribbean basin US diplomacy and the threat of US force kept in power conservative tyrants who gave every impression of looking after the interests of Washington more diligently than the interests of their own people.

The US-backed Bay of Pigs invasion of Cuba in 1962 and the US-led invasion of the Dominican Republic in 1965 reminded the world that Washington was still willing to use force in defence of its interests. Until comparatively recently, however, the weight of United States power was felt little in the south of South America. In Argentina, as in Iran, the legend that the British were pulling the strings of power remained in popular currency long after British political and economic influence had waned in the region. Then in 1973 the overthrow by a military putsch of the left-wing government of President Salvador Allende in Chile, with the active co-operation of Washington, brought home to Latin Americans that United States power was sufficient to reach into every corner of the continent. It reminded all the governments, the anti-communist ones who were delighted to see Allende dead as well as the others, of their common Latin American identity.

As United States power grew, so sentiment in Latin America swelled against that country's meddling in the region's affairs. But the sentiment which drew Latin Americans together in the face of an excessively powerful neighbour seldom resulted in joint political and diplomatic action to forestall it. It became clear that Washington's interests were totally at odds with any moves towards political unity among the Latin American governments and United States diplomacy was almost always successful in thwarting the ill-concerted efforts of the Latin American governments to present a united front to United States policies. From the end of the last century on, the Latin Americans struggled to put together some sort of common platform for their own deliberations: they were unsuccessful because they could not, or would not, resist the pressure of successive United States governments to

34

take part. There blossomed a whole series of institutions which tended to have 'Pan-American' or 'Inter-American' in their titles and which generally represented successful attempts by US diplomats to prevent the Latin Americans taking any initiative of their own which Washington was not in a position to monitor and, if need be, crush. The Inter-American Development Bank, a bank whose founding shareholders were individual governments in the western hemisphere, made sure that despite the requirements of its own statutes it made few loans or none to nationalist governments of which Washington disapproved, such as those of Juan Velasco in Peru in the late 1960s, Salvador Allende in the early 1970s and the Sandinistas in Nicaragua in the 1980s; the Inter-American Press Association did what it could for the freedom of newspapers and magazines provided they were not left-wing. There is an Inter-American Tropical Tuna Commission, a Pan-American Development Association, an Inter-American Music Council, an Inter-American Bar Association, a Pan-American Association of Ophthalmology and an Inter-American Commercial Arbitration Commission, to name but a few, all of which have their headquarters in the United States.

The father of them all was the Pan-American Union whose origins lay in an international conference called by governments in Washington in 1889. It was rechristened the Organisation of American States (OAS) after the Second World War and has regularly and dismissively been referred to by left-wingers as 'the United States ministry of the colonies'.

At the height of US power in the hemisphere in 1962, the United States was able to engineer a vote which suspended from membership of the OAS the government of Cuba even though several OAS members had no quarrel with the Castro government. Three years later the United States staged a military operation to prevent the reinstatement in the Dominican Republic of a constitutional government which was too uncomfortably nationalistic for Washington. The invasion was camouflaged by being carried out under the supposed aegis of the OAS whose less powerful members, including the Stroessner dictatorship in Paraguay, provided a few contingents of soldiers. The aim was to give the false impression that what was to all intents and purposes a US intervention had been an international operation.

In the late 1970s President Carter, to his great credit, inaugurated a period in which for the first time human rights became one of the criteria by which the United States shaped its policies to the region. It cost him the co-operation of the military regimes and did not glean him much goodwill from the perennially suspicious Latin American left. As he did not present a major threat to any government of the region, his presidency did not do as much as earlier ones to enhance Latin Americans' sense of identity against an outside foe.

It was not until the 1980s that the region's governments managed finally to present some semblance of a common front to Washington. Throughout the 1970s the governments of the region borrowed heavily from foreign bankers. As the price of oil went up those countries which had no oil of their own borrowed in order to pay their bills for imported oil. The Latin American countries which did have their own oil and thus were much better off because of the rise in the oil prices borrowed as well, for the fun of it. There is nothing a banker enjoys more than lending cash to someone who does not need it. By 1982 the combined total weight of $300 000 millionsworth of foreign debt had become too much for the Latin Americans to support, and Mexico took the momentous step of stopping its payments of interest and repayments of capital. In the aftermath of this decision, the other Latin American debtors jockeyed for position and favour with the creditors of the industrialised countries. The latter were themselves keeping a strictly united front against the Latin Americans. But as the debt load increased, passing $400 000 million in 1987, the governments of Latin America were gradually forced into precarious collaboration with each other, conscious that their debts gave them power over a set of more and more nervous bankers. Though the cohesion of the Latin American creditors towards their Western creditors was weak compared to the unity the Western borrowers were able to maintain against them, the foreign debt crisis did serve to remind the Latin Americans of their shared identity and their shared problems. Slowly a rough Latin American consensus emerged to the effect that no country would devote so much of its foreign currency to the payments of its obligations that its economies were forced to stop growing or its people obliged to starve. The consensus has been a ragged one, and not comparable to the neat agreements on precise interest rate percentages and repayment periods that the creditors ceaselessly work out. But ragged though it is, it is still powerful enough to frighten the industrial countries.

So in the late 1980s the Latin Americans find themselves in a situation which is still extraordinary and complicated. In most of the republics the gap between rich and poor is wide and is not narrowing. Like the Arabs, the Latin Americans have a great many things in common but the vast area over which they are scattered militates against their easily coming together in one nation. Only occasionally can they agree on a joint action on specific policies.

Being a Latin American, like being a European, is a state of mind. It is never a recipe for uniformity.

CHAPTER TWO

# THE MILITARY

*If I'd known my son was going to become president of the republic I'd have taught him to read.*

MOTHER OF AN ANONYMOUS BOLIVIAN GENERAL

———

The image that I most vividly retain of the Chilean putsch in Santiago in 1973 is not that of death and bloodshed but of celebration and fear.

The evening of that mild spring day, Tuesday 11 September, General Augusto Pinochet had been in power for a few hours. The guests were assembled in the main hall of the Hotel Carrera, a sumptuous room three storeys high, stone-floored and with a splendid carpeted staircase with polished brass handrails which rose from the main entrance to the reception desk on the first floor. The light of the elegant modern chandeliers was reflected from the black glass which covered the walls and from the pillars of polished cream stone which rose in the centre of the room. The glass itself was etched and coloured with elegant and idealistic representations of the arrival in Chile of Pedro de Valdivia, the first conquistador, in the sixteenth century. The steel shutters which protected the great windows onto the plaza had been drawn and were veiled by the light white cotton curtains which hung from ceiling to floor. Despite the hardness of the floor and the coldness of the walls, there was a sense of warmth. There was joy and cosiness. The new regime had decreed a curfew. The doors were barred. No one left and no one entered. The shutters and the curtains kept the world out. The glistening and gleaming Carrera was a world on its own that night. We might as well all have been on the other side of the world, at sea, perhaps, on the *Normandie* or the *Queen Mary*, cutting smoothly across some calm patch of the North Atlantic Ocean.

People sat around on the sofas or at the little copper-topped tables. They talked animatedly, the suave men and the elegant ladies. They laughed and joked and drank noisily, the sound of their celebration bouncing and echoing off the shiny walls. Every so often there was an expectant hush when the television came up with a *bando*, some new message from the new masters of Chile. When it was ended there were cheers, more champagne corks popped and from ladies' slippers toasts were drunk to Pinochet and his brave companions.

In the corner the service door opened from time to time and groups of waiters peered timidly out. The juxtaposition of the stylish carousers and the apprehensive serving staff was dramatic and served like nothing else to bring home the social impact of the putsch above and beyond the patriotic and martial music that the radio and the television were broadcasting. The waiters and the rest of those below stairs knew what military rule was going to bring and they were afraid. History proved their fears were justified.

I had spent most of the Tuesday, from ten o'clock in the morning till quarter past four in the afternoon, in the British embassy round the corner from the Moneda palace and the Carrera. The embassy was on the first floor of a solid office building whose ground floor housed the local branch of the Bank of London and South America. I had gone there with Stewart Russell, the Reuters man, in the hope of finding some way of getting a fuller story of the putsch out to the world after the military had cut off all telecommunications. The embassy could not help us but by the time we had established that, the firing was so heavy in the streets that we thought it safer to stay indoors. From time to time Stewart and I went down to the ground floor and peered through the bronze gates which barred the entrance at the troops in the calle Bandera as they glanced nervously up at the tall buildings for snipers. Now and again a stray ricochet would ping against the gates.

To their shame, various members of the embassy staff and their wives who were with us made no secret of their jubilation that Allende had been driven from power and the military had taken over. Throughout the late morning and into the early afternoon as we ate the tinned food the diplomats provided us for lunch, we heard the occasional shot of a sniper on our roof a few floors above who was bravely and hopelessly holding out against the tanks and the troops in the streets. By the sound of it he had only a small calibre weapon, perhaps a .22, and in the afternoon a helicopter came over and killed him. I was never able to find out who he was, but his bravery lives after him. When the firing died down Stewart and I walked back to our hotels with our hands in the air.

That night the guests slept in the sub-basement for safety's sake. When we went back to our rooms we watched the flames still leaping from the Moneda diagonally across the plaza. It had been bombed by the British-built Hunter jets of the Chilean air force just after Tuesday midday; and less than two hours later Salvador Allende had died resisting the army's assault. The elected civilian government, albeit an ill-disciplined and turbulent one, had been overthrown by an army which had had the reputation of being non-political and obedient. Many people were to be tortured and killed. Many poor Chileans, who had seen Allende's election as their hope for a better life, were to see themselves pushed back into hunger, their children deprived of the better start which Allende's programme of free school milk and improved educational chances had begun to offer them.

The presidential apartments, where I had several times talked and eaten with Allende, burnt for days smouldering down to a dark red glow inside the sober grey walls of the Moneda.

## Conflicting faces of the military

The images of the military in Latin America veer between the comic, the sinister and the corrupt and there is much truth in them.

The archetype of the Latin American military as buffoon is surely General Mariano Melgarejo who ruled Bolivia between December 1865 and 1871 and whose exploits have been set down by the Bolivian historian Tomás O'Connor d'Arlach.

Melgarejo, he records, was a great Francophile and an enthusiastic drinker. One midnight he sounded the alarm and had the army parade in the city square in La Paz. Everyone was mystified.

'Soldiers,' he cried out in the gloom, 'the integrity of France is menaced by Prussia. He who menaces France, menaces civilisation and liberty. I shall protect the French, who are our best friends and whom I so love. You are going to swim the Ocean with me. But take care to keep your powder dry.'

Under a great straw hat and mounted on his Chilean charger Holofernes, he swept unsteadily off. Before long his ministers caught up with him and asked him what route he would be taking to the Franco–Prussian War.

'Down the dirt road,' he replied grandly. At that, it started to rain heavily and the General gradually sobered up.

On another occasion he had Holofernes brought into a banquet so that the guests could drink its health. After the toast he ordered one distinguished guest to lead it back to its stable and give it its hay.

Once when Melgarejo was receiving a foreign envoy at the palace he had his escort form up so he could demonstrate the marvellous discipline of his army. He ordered the men to march straight out of the room. Through the French windows they went, onto the balcony and over into the street many feet below.

O'Connor d'Arlach tells of the time Melgarejo was reviewing his army when it became overcast and thundery.

'Soldiers,' he commanded, 'not even the elements must pit themselves against the power of the great invincible army of December and its captain-general. Clear away these clouds with the smoke from the powder of your weapons!'

The army fired into the sky and before long the clouds did in fact clear. His reputation with his troops soared.

But for every Melgarejo there is a Pinochet, scowling out at the world through dark glasses, as in his first official photograph after the putsch of September 1973. For every funny Bolivian story there are scores which tell of Uruguayan officers drowning their captives in bathfuls of shit or of Salvadorean troops disembowelling and gouging the eyes out of their victims before throwing the bodies out at El Playón, the recognised tip for corpses in the petrified volcanic lava a few miles north of San Salvador.

Uruguay, up to the 1973 coup, had been a country with a very strong civilian tradition. That did not stop the military taking over and starting a reign of terror, as one prisoner recounted:

Another day it was my turn for the *plantón* [forced standing] treatment, along with two others: one man, who, judging from his voice, was over 60; and a young woman, not much more than a girl. The *plantón* involves standing with your legs apart. It is unwise to fall, but standing like that for hours is very difficult. At dusk, the old man fell and three of them began to interrogate him. They practically drove him out of his mind. They said shocking things to him about his wife and daughter-in-law and about what they were going to do to him next. I gathered, from overhearing the interrogation, that the man had two sons, both fine men and fine workers. At nightfall, the old man 'betrayed' them. The young woman wept slowly.

A year later, I learned that all three had been together in the same jail and I was able to round off the story. The old man really did go mad in the end. He prayed all day and asked his sons to do the same. They never spoke to him again, but they gave him their blankets on cold nights so that he would not freeze to death, for the soldiers treated him very badly and, on top of everything else, mocked him – this was his reward for collaborating with them . . .

The night of the dogs was one of the worst nights. They suspended three people, one woman and two men, in a corner. They hung the woman by her hair and the men under the arms. Their feet were four or five centimetres above the ground. The dogs stood underneath them, barking. I could visualise the three of them trembling with fear. The woman (fortunately for her) fainted. The dogs never stopped barking. At dawn, they asked them if they had anything to say to the commanding officer. No one replied. They brought the woman round by throwing water on her, and asked her the same question. She did not reply either. They took her down and threw her on the floor. The dogs attacked her.

What that man recounted about Uruguay in November 1976 had, and in some cases still has, its parallels in Chile, or Paraguay, Argentina or Guatemala.

The question of military corruption was put with classical succinctness by Alvaro Obregón, a leader of the Army of the North in the Mexican revolution of 1910. 'There is,' he said, 'no general who can withstand a bombardment of 50000 pesos.' Military corruption is everywhere in Latin America and the examples are endless.

'Every military man who has occupied the Presidency since 1970 has ended his term a millionaire several times over,' wrote the Guatemalan weekly *This Week*.

In Paraguay General Alfredo Stroessner, who took power in 1954, has made the distribution of opportunities for corruption a key element in the maintenance of his control over the officer corps. Military fortunes are made on a franchise from the general to smuggle whisky or other consumer goods into the territory of one or other of Paraguay's neighbours, or to distribute in the Paraguayan capital cars stolen from the city streets in Brazil.

In institutionalised military dictatorships corruption can go on from one generation to another. In Nicaragua the Somoza dynasty, father Anastasio (Tacho) and two sons, Luis and Tachito, controlled the country through the National Guard, established during the United States occupation. When Tachito and his family were finally ousted by the Sandinista revolution of 1979, their fortune was estimated at £500 million. Arturo Cruz, president of the Central Bank after Tachito's fall and later a supporter of the Contras, commented, 'For years Somoza ran this country like a private enterprise. It was a mechanism to produce hard currency to invest abroad.'

In the 1980s, however, the rise of the drug traffic, particularly marijuana and cocaine, from Latin America to markets in the United States, Canada and Europe has lifted military corruption onto a plane which even General Obregón would be hard put to recognise. Marijuana and cocaine have produced an avalanche of money which has swept through the countryside of the Andean and Caribbean regions, destroying the probity of all but a few of the officers who control that countryside.

In Bolivia, for instance, cocaine has become more valuable than any legal export crop. Leaves from 100000 hectares of coca bush provide the raw material for 40 per cent of the world's consumption of the drug. The coca plantations that have from time immemorial produced leaves for the Andean peasant to chew so he could dull the pains of cold and hunger now produce narcotics worth thousands of millions of pounds in the richer consumer countries. A coup d'état on 17 July 1980 put into power in Bolivia a military government, led by General Luis García Meza, which was intimately involved with the cocaine trade.

Colonel Luis Arce Gómez became interior minister in García Meza's government and Colonel Ariel Coca education minister. Arce Gómez and another colonel owned an airfreight firm, one of whose aircraft was found to have 300 kilos of cocaine aboard. He was later indicted by grand juries in the United States on drugs charges. Coca was also a prominent trafficker: his brother was arrested in Panama with 100 kilos of cocaine. During the García Meza dictatorship Roberto Suárez, the country's most prominent trafficker, offered to pay off the whole of the country's foreign debt of $3.8 billion in return for special terms in the courts.

## The historical role of the military

The military have had a particularly privileged position in Latin America ever since the region became Latin. The two principal colonisers, Spain and Portugal, embarked on conquest for various reasons – glory, power and riches for the sovereigns and the soldier who carried out their orders and the spreading of the Catholic faith. But there was no doubt that it was to be a military conquest in which the native people would be reduced to submission and the conquered area transformed into an extension of the realms of the Catholic European monarchs. In that way, the Spanish and Portuguese colonisation effort was different from much of the effort undertaken in America by the English. It was, in particular, different from the sort of effort which was undertaken by the Puritans who left England to escape from the orthodoxies of the English established church and found the society which was eventually to mature into the Protestant United States in 1776.

At the time of independence in the first decades of the last century, the states which emerged from the break-up of the Spanish empire were in large measure created by military men at the behest of local oligarchies. These oligarchies felt they would do better being independent of Spain than if they continued as subjects of Spain whose government sought to control and regulate their activities, particularly their economic activities. José de San Martín, 'the Liberator' who freed much of southern South America up to Peru, and Simon Bolivar of Caracas, who freed what is now Venezuela, Colombia, Panama and Ecuador, were typical of many others whose statues are to be found in heroic poses in city squares up and down the continent. The states of Spanish America were in great part forged by generals; some had previous military experience in the armies of Spain, others were homegrown fighters. John Lynch in his book *The Spanish American Revolutions 1808–1826* describes José Antonio Páez, a *llanero* or man from the plains of the Orinoco River and the most famous of the latter sort of

45

warrior that Venezuela produced, in the following terms:

> The *llanero* warrior had now acquired a huge fortune and vast landed wealth; he was an entrepreneur in commerce and agriculture, and, though his greatest passion was gambling and cock-fighting, he was trying hard to improve himself. 'As a man,' noted the British consul, 'he possesses a naturally strong mind, but from being totally uneducated, is extremely diffident of himself when in the society of others endowed with the advantages of education. Feeling this inferiority, and anxious to improve, he has, within these very few years, applied himself to reading and writing; which acquirement until then he was totally ignorant of.'

When the Spaniards, or *peninsulares*, were finally defeated, the *criollos* or creoles, men of the type of San Martín, Bolivar and Páez had power and prestige in their hands. Some were offered the crown of new monarchies in the New World, some were out-manoeuvred, made bitter and went into exile.

Others continued on in the lands they knew ruling as *caudillos*, unmolested by and uncaring about the governments in the national capitals, paternalistically ruling over the local people. Rather disingenuously, Páez once wrote to Bolivar, 'I do not know why, but the people bring me all their problems – how to build a house, whom to marry, how to settle a family dispute , and what seeds to plant.' Páez, of course, knew exactly why the people came to him as they did. He was the centre of power, knowledge and influence; there were no political parties to represent them and apart from the clergy, if there were any clergy, no one else to give them help and advice. There can be no doubt, however, that military men were the creators of the modern states of Spanish America, or better, the agents of those members of an emerging middle class who wanted a new society which offered them greater opportunities.

In one or two cases in Spanish America the soldiers who brought into being the new nations were anxious for genuine popular government to take root. In the Banda Oriental, the eastern shore of the River Plate which was later to be known as Uruguay, the man mainly responsible for independence was a local soldier named José Gervasio Artigas. Artigas was a reformer who wanted some of the great cattle estates to be broken up for the benefit of the poor and who was in favour of emancipation for black slaves. This, as Lynch quotes a British naval officer as saying, did not endear him to the oligarchy.

> There is no doubt considerable fermentation has been excited amongst the slaves by his proclamations and the encouragement he holds forth and it is extremely probable very many of them will escape and join his army . . . The general feeling amongst the people of property and any consideration not only on this side of the Plata but on the opposite one, is against Artigas, whose popularity, although considerable, is entirely confined to the lower orders of the community and arises from those very causes which make him most dreaded by the higher, namely in not only permitting but encouraging every excess and disorder amongst his followers.

A British traveller had this description of the founder of Uruguay at the height of his powers:

> What do you think I saw? His Excellency the Señor Protector of half of the New World sitting on the head of an ox beside a bonfire on the muddy soil of his ranch eating barbecued meat and drinking gin from a cow's horn! A dozen ragged officers surrounded him.

Uruguayans who, until the 1970s, had been less subject to military rule than their neighbours took pride in the more humane legacy left to them by Artigas. In the majority of countries, however, militarism was and remained a curse. Lynch comments on the situation in Spanish America after the wars of independence were over.

> The size and expense of armies were out of all proportion to their function, particularly after the last Spanish bases had been removed; for it needed little insight to appreciate that European invaders would have little chance of survival in independent Latin America. So the new states were left with virtual armies of occupation, whose function was principally the welfare of their own members. To disband them was difficult because it was expensive. In the immediate

aftermath of the war, the Colombian army stood at 25–30000, and its budget represented three-quarters of the total expenditure of Santander's government.

In Brazil, as Leslie Bethell recounts in his *Cambridge History of Latin America*, history was different. The colonial power of Portugal was not overthrown by locally born officers like that of Spain. The Royal Navy escorted the Portuguese royal family from Lisbon away from the threat of capture by the invading French in November 1807. It was a nightmare voyage for King João VI, his mad mother, his wife Carlota Joaquina and their two sons. They were crowded, hungry, thirsty and plagued with parasites. The ladies had to cut off their hair because of the lice, and changes of clothes had to be fashioned out of sheets and blankets provided by the sailors. But on 22 January 1808, João and his court landed in the Brazilian port of Bahia, the first reigning monarch of Europe to have set foot on the American continent. The court was established in Rio de Janeiro where, in 1815, Portugal's former colony was raised to the status of a kingdom in its own right, equal in rights to Portugal itself. Dom João lived on in Rio till he returned to Lisbon in 1821.

A year later his son Dom Pedro was crowned Constitutional Emperor and Perpetual Defender of Brazil and the monarchy survived till the second emperor abdicated in 1889. Brazil was spared much of the military rule by *pronunciamiento* that the Spanish-speakers suffered under the successors of the generals who beat the Spaniards. Though Brazil was ruled by generals from 1964 to 1985, it has never quite been the playground for the military that countries like Argentina and Guatemala have been.

In general, however, the military throughout the region have a far more effective and immediate grip on civil society than anywhere in Western Europe today, a grip more effective even than that exercised by the military in the two superpowers.

## The caudillo

The military have also provided the greatest number, though not all, of those most Hispanic of figures, the *caudillo*. The *caudillo* is the strongman who makes the law up as he goes along, imposing his will and drawing supporters to him with the force of his personality. The title is considered an honourable one in the Spanish-speaking world. General Franco, who emerged victorious at the end of the Spanish Civil War and who ruled Spain with a rod of iron till his death, was happy to be called a *caudillo*. 'Francisco Franco, by the grace of God, Caudillo of Spain', ran the inscription on the coinage during his period in power. At all times and under all regimes the *caudillo* has been present in Latin America: Cortés and Pizarro in colonial times, Bolivar, Páez, San Martín and many more at the time of independence, Perón and Castro in our own time.

The *caudillo* is the man who rules. He can do so because the structures of society are not, as in Britain and Scandinavia, strong enough to hold him back. Cortés went ahead and conquered Mexico because it was outside the orbit of Spain; and the same was true for Pizarro in Peru. But once the power of Spain and Portugal was established, the opportunities for that sort of self-aggrandisement were fewer. Such opportunities returned when Spanish America was freeing itself from Spanish rule and continued in the weak and often chaotically organised states which came after.

Antonio López de Santa Anna was *caudillo* of Mexico for two decades from 1833, occupying the presidency or manipulating it through puppets. He naturally became immensely rich through protection rackets, the sale of offices and contracts and he owned nearly 50000 acres of land on which he grazed 40000 head of cattle. He had himself titled 'His Most Serene Highness' and signed documents 'Santa Anna, Saviour of the Fatherland, General of Divison, Knight Grand Cross of the Royal and Distinguished Spanish Order of Charles III, President of the Mexican Republic and the Distinguished Order of Guadalupe.' His bodyguard was called 'The Lancers of the Supreme Power' and numbered 1200 men. The feast day of Saint Anne became a public holiday.

In 1838 France went to war with Mexico over a ridiculous episode ten years previously in which hungry Mexican soldiers had guzzled the stock-in-trade of a French pastrycook and not paid. In one skirmish in what became known as the Pastry War, the great Santa Anna's left leg was injured and had to be amputated below the knee. It was mummified and buried respectfully. Six years later the leg was exhumed and taken ceremoniously to Mexico City where, in the presence of the army, the cabinet, the diplomatic corps and the congress and amid speeches, songs and eulogies of the *caudillo* it was placed in an urn and lodged at the top of a column in the

Santa Fé cemetery. Santa Anna was later responsible for the battle of the Alamo, the consequent loss of the Mexican state of Texas to English-speaking settlers and its eventual absorption into the United States. His rule was one of unmitigated disaster for Mexico. There have been many like Santa Anna in Latin America.

The character of the Latin American military and the military's relationship with the rest of society, fixed over the centuries, subsists. If society in the region is a racialist one, in which the whites and the near-whites tend to do better than people of any other colour, this is in some measure due to the fact that Latin American armies are carrying out the precepts that were given to them in colonial times of subduing the natives. If the society is one where the small locally-born bourgeoisies prosper at the expense of the vast majority of the population, this is in some measure because the soldiers are obeying the commands they were given by the forebears of those bourgeoisies at the time of independence. The military have, as in most parts of the world, been custodians of the status quo. Those countries in which the military traditions are most deeply rooted – Guatemala, Bolivia, El Salvador – are often the ones in which the development of society and evolution away from racialist attitudes have come more slowly. Countries in which the military have played a more subordinate role to the civilian government – Costa Rica, and Chile and Uruguay till the coups of 1973, Venezuela since the fall of the last military dictator in 1958 – have generally produced more enlightened societies.

There have, of course, been many exceptions to this general rule. There have certainly been generals with reforming instincts, *caudillos* who wanted to escape the too close embrace of the middle classes and become 'fathers of the fatherland' in the spirit of Artigas.

*Argentina*  Juan Domingo Perón who rose to power in Argentina in 1945 was the best known. During his first ten years in power he did his best to smash the power of the Argentine oligarchy. He also fashioned the working class into an unorganised movement which owed strict personal allegiance to him and which, in turn, received Perón's support against those employers who did not make their peace with the *caudillo*.

He combined his social ideas with a large measure of nationalism and xenophobia against Britain and the US in particular.

An admiral who served in his cabinet summed up the feelings of many who supported the rise of Perón,

> The Argentine Republic was one of the most hated backward countries in Latin America in social welfare and labour legislation – at least in its effectiveness.
>
> In all the great crises that nations face, a providential saviour always appears who owes a great deal to those who made his rise possible and necessary.
>
> In our situation the appearance of a colonel, then unknown outside the Army, excited first the attention and then the support of millions of his fellow citizens. And what was most extraordinary: a man of arms succeeded in being believed by the labouring masses.

Perón was overthrown and sent into exile in 1955 but won elections to become president again in 1973. He died the next year, his supporters divided, disgruntled and disorganised, and he left a legacy of total political and organisational chaos to his third wife María Estela, a former nightclub dancer who had gone under the name of Isabelita. She proved incapable of governing and was in her turn overthrown by conservative generals in 1976. Peronism, despite the fact that it continues to be an incoherent, though still powerful, political force in Argentina, has brought more confusion than long-term benefit to the poorest Argentines who were left leaderless – even orphaned – and disorganised after Perón's death.

*Peru* A similar phenomenon of hopes raised and then disappointed by military men occurred in Peru where General Juan Velasco Alvarado took power in 1968. Velasco – known as El Chino, 'the Chinaman' – and General Francisco Morales Bermúdez, who overthrew him in 1975, set out with a policy of reforming and modernising a backward and deeply divided society. The experience ended in débâcle, not in the grand emotional débâcle that characterised the last years of Peronism, but in the dull realisation that it would take more than the skill and will of one soldier or a group of comrades to lift the humble of Peru up from destitution. In their book *Peru 1890–1977*, Rosemary Thorp and Geoffrey Bertram are tart about Velasco,

> The military regime, we believe, correctly identified a number of the key problems for Peruvian development, but

failed to tackle them from any consistent political or ideological stance – a trait which led one journal to report a
major policy speech by President Velasco under the apt
headline 'Neither Left, Right, nor Centre'.

Despite the best of intentions no Latin American officer has
succeeded in carrying out real and lasting programmes of social
reform. Whether they have liked it or not, the armies in Latin
America have continued to protect the middle class which called
them into being at the beginning of the last century in order to get
rid of Spanish rule.

## Boundary wars in Latin America

The task of protecting the middle class has been made all the easier
by the fact that Latin American armies have only very rarely had to
protect the territory of their own countries against foreign
invaders. The boundaries of the republics which were set up at the
time of independence have changed remarkably little – certainly in
comparison with the almost frenetic frontier adjustments that have
taken place over the past century in Europe. There were few major
wars in which Latin American states lost territory to other states. In
1879, Chile went to war with Peru and Bolivia over the control of
the very profitable nitrate deposits in the Atacama Desert. As a
result the defeated countries lost territory and the Bolivians were
turned out of the port of Cobija and their only outlet to the Pacific.
Since that time they have tended to ascribe their mountainous
economic problems to the fact that they are landlocked, but they
have acquired neither the diplomatic skill nor the military power to
dislodge the Chileans.

*Paraguay*   The other two wars involved Paraguay. Between 1864
and 1870 the *caudillo* of Paraguay, Francisco Solano López, waged a
war against his two most powerful neighbours, Argentina and
Brazil, who together with Uruguay made up the Triple Alliance.
An admirer of Napoleon, Solano López saw himself as a man of
destiny. War could have been avoided had he not had his navy
attack and capture a Brazilian ship in the Paraguay River. Nor did
he have to have the ship's ensign made into a rug for his office. But
he did commit both these, and other, provocative acts. For a time
the war went well for him as the three allies struggled to co-ordinate

their efforts. The Brazilians did not have much fighting spirit and some of the Argentine recruits arrived at the front in chains. The Uruguayans sent only a nominal detachment to fight. But all three countries, particularly the bigger ones, had reserves that the Paraguayans could not count on. The rank and file of the Paraguayan army went barefoot. One English observer of the war noted that among the Paraguayan artillery train were two guns produced in Seville, one, the San Gabriel, dating from 1671 and the other, the San Juan de Dios, from 1684. Another English writer said the greater part of the Paraguayan artillery 'were like the guns which do duty as posts on Woolwich Common'.

Solano López' victories could not last and, despite a manic resistance by the Paraguayans, the allied troops flooded into the country. The Marshal-President was killed after the battle of Cerro Corá when he was pierced in the belly by a Brazilian lancer. A lancer also killed his son Juan Francisco, at fifteen already a full colonel. They were mourned by Eliza Lynch, his Irish mistress who was with him at the last and who later died in poverty in Paris.

His last words were 'Muero con mi patria' ('I die with my country'). He was almost literally right. The war cost Paraguay half its population: 220 000 Paraguayans died in battle or of disease and hunger and 221 000 survived. Of the survivors only 28 000 were men and there were therefore four women of marriageable age to every man. It took generations for the balance between the two sexes to be restored. A prosperous and advanced country, which had built the first railway in South America and which had the chance of becoming a big power in the region, was reduced to a pitiable state.

That did not prevent Paraguay going to war again in 1932, this time with Bolivia over control of the hot wilderness of the Chaco where there was supposed to be oil. The combatants were wrenched apart in 1935 by mediators, to the great disappointment of the Paraguayan army which was gaining the upper hand. Nevertheless 36 000 Paraguayans lay dead. After both wars the exhausted country lapsed into a period of political anarchy in which governments succeeded one another like men coming through revolving doors. There were three presidents in 1911, four in 1912, three in 1924, 1932 and 1948 and four in 1949. In 1954 an officer who had fought in the Chaco War came to power. At the time of writing, General Alfredo Stroessner was still the dictator of Paraguay.

Despite these savage conflicts, full-scale wars have been relatively rare and border changes have, as a general rule, been small and achieved by diplomatic intrigue rather than by force of arms. Brazil, with a well-trained and efficient foreign service, is said to have acquired territory from every one of its neighbours but this has been done generally by non-violent means.

## Conflicts involving foreign powers

The absence of grand cross-border wars of the sort that Europeans have gone in for from time immemorial has had two effects. Latin American societies have generally not undergone the great shake-ups that war has brought to European societies, and the military have been able to concentrate on the task of making sure revolutionaries did not carry out their revolutionary plans.

None of the Latin American states was involved in the First World War and, although many Latin American governments declared war on the Axis when it was clear that the Allies were close to victory, only Brazil and Mexico went as far as to send troops to the war effort. The Brazilian Expeditionary Force, the FEB, played a useful, but scarcely major, role in the Allied invasion of Italy, fighting at Monte Cassino and at the end receiving the surrender of a German division. The Mexicans sent an air force squadron to the Philippines which went into action over Taiwan.

The Cuban forces faced and defeated a US threat at the Bay of Pigs in 1961 and supported left-wing governments in Angola and Ethiopia. The Sandinistas in Nicaragua are emulating the example of the Bay of Pigs as they fight the terrorism of the Contras. In neither Cuba nor Nicaragua, however, has Washington committed its own forces, preferring to fight through proxies and rely on expatriate personnel supported indirectly from the United States. To say that is not, of course, to decry the bravery and skill of the Cuban or the Nicaraguan armies. During the Falklands affair, the one recent occasion when a Latin American army was called upon to fight against a Western army trained for a modern war, the outcome showed up in excruciating detail the shortcomings of a Latin American army organised for internal repression.

## 'National security'

The armies of the region have then seldom been distracted by either local or world conflicts from their primary role of maintaining society as it has traditionally been. In the 1960s and 1970s in many countries, notably Brazil, this mission of preserving the status quo in society was clothed with intellectual pretension in the form of doctrines of 'national security'. The doctrines were worked on at military academies up and down the region but nowhere more assiduously than at the Escola Superior de Guerra, or Higher School of War, founded in Brazil in 1949. The interests of the state were presented as being paramount and sacred and therefore worthy of every sort of protection against 'subversion'. Proper security, it was argued, depended not just on the defence of national frontiers but also on the exploitation of natural resources and the progressive enrichment of all sectors of society. Some said that the exploitation of local potential demanded an alliance with international capital and the multinational companies, others distrusted foreign bankers and entrepreneurs. The proponents of the national security doctrines did not, however, call into question the right of the local oligarchies to continue at the helm of the nation. Nor did they consider that the modernisation of their societies in accordance with European or US patterns demanded a degree of effective democratisation. That would have horrified the ruling élites in Latin America. The military in Brazil went as far as to overthrow the elected President João Goulart in 1964 in the interests of 'national security'. Two years later 'national security' was again invoked by the military dictator General Humberto Castelo Branco, who introduced legislation which stripped every last vestige of real authority from the congress and ushered in two decades during which Brazil was a police state where protesters ran the risk of assassination or imprisonment and the most revolting and degrading punishments. The Brazilian experiment with a 'national security' state was made all the more telling and attractive to the military in Spanish America because of a number of coincidental factors. By the early 1970s the country, which was already the regional superpower, was enjoying economic growth rates of more than 10 per cent a year, as well as having a close relationship with the United States (whose government had welcomed, and perhaps even helped to instigate, the military putsch of 1964), and seemed to be providing a model of stability, prosperity and modernisation.

In the developed world, the interests of the bankers who were lending and exporters who were selling to Brazil at great profit muted criticism of the atrocities which the military and police were at liberty to carry out. It was not until the onset of Latin America's debt crisis in the early 1980s, when the borrowing strategies followed by authoritarian military governments – and some civilian ones – were shown to have been wildly misguided and to be producing national bankruptcy, that 'national security' fell out of favour.

## Accountability of the military

While the military have been protecting the middle classes they have been protecting themselves. Throughout most of Latin America, with or without any intellectual underpinning, the armed forces are a law to themselves. In many republics the constitution specifically states that a civilian president shall have no authority to appoint the senior officers of the armed forces, this task being carried out by internal deliberation within the ranks. Soldiers, too, are subject to their own set of laws and do not answer to the civilian courts. And the military tribunals are there not just to try soldiers on military offences. Civilians thought guilty of offences against the forces are taken to these tribunals for their punishment.

In El Salvador and Guatemala, in the six years from 1979, 100 000 civilians were killed by the armed forces. Some of those civilians, notably the four church women who died near the international airport in El Salvador in 1981, were citizens of the United States, whose government is the main ally of Salvadorean military. Yet for none of those killings, the vast majority of which were acts of terror rather than acts of self-defence by soldiers, has a member of the armed forces been given the sort of punishment which natural justice would demand.

Only in Argentina has the civilian power tried in a sweeping way to assert its authority over the military. President Raúl Alfonsín was elected to office at the end of 1984, after six years in which the military had used terrorism of every sort to crush their enemies. They had also started and lost a military adventure in the Falklands. They had been shown to be both cruel and incompetent. Justice, and a very vocal claque of relatives of the victims, demanded that they be punished for what were, by any definition, crimes. Yet Alfonsín, conscious of the physical power of the military and of the strength of militarism in a country whose children are taught from their earliest days to revere the name of San Martín and revere the army, hesitated. Initially he wanted the military themselves to use their own judicial system to sit in judgement on the military malefactors. But the Supreme Council of the Armed Forces refused to move. So on 22 April 1985, before civilian judges, there opened a trial which was to conclude eight months later with heavy sentences for the senior generals and admirals. But during the military dictatorship it had been the practice for commanders to involve even the most junior officers in atrocities so that all were implicated in the deeds of the juntas. Few professionals in the armed forces were totally innocent of misdeeds, a fact that made it impossible for a civilian government to bring all the guilty to justice without risking the complete collapse of the country's defence system. In the end thousands had to be let off. In his summing-up the state prosecutor, Julio Strassera, declared, 'The trial has meant, for those of us who have had the painful privilege of following closely, a descent into the most terrible depths of the human soul, where misery, degradation and horror have been registered with such intensity that it could scarcely have been imagined or understood'. The code of military justice is only the last line of defence for the armed forces.

## Defence spending

The first line of defence is money, and the military generally make sure that they have good access to the national budgets. The Latin American states between them spend about $20 000 million a year on their armed forces. Some governments are low spenders, like Brazil and Mexico who spend no more than about 0.6 per cent of the annual Gross National Product on the military. At the other end of the scale are Argentina, Chile and Peru who have been spending up to 10 per cent of the national wealth every year on the armed forces. With civilian governments in power in Argentina and Peru there has, happily, been a tendency for military spending there to decrease. In Central America, suffering under the impact of nine years of war, military costs are clearly going up. In most circumstances the generals are able to get the local currency they need for domestic spending. They also clearly get the foreign currency that they need for imported weapons even when that foreign currency is, as now, very scarce. As Latin America staggers under a foreign debt which has become virtually unmanageable, scholars have estimated that a minimum of 9 per cent of the foreign debt owed or guaranteed by governments was contracted for arms purchases. From 1970 to 1983 a total of more than $20000 million was spent on imported weapons which created an annual bill for interest of $2300 million. Money spent on the import of arms was not available for other, more productive, uses and that was clearly a gross error in a region where such poverty exists. Economists also argue that money spent on arms purchases has fuelled inflation in Latin America, in that governments spent money they printed themselves without providing goods and services for the population to buy. With its strong military tradition, with military governments having been in power for more than a decade and with the country coming to the brink of war with Chile over the control of the Beagle Channel near Cape Horn in 1979, Argentina has been perhaps the most profligate spender. Perhaps as much as a quarter of the government's foreign debt seems to have been run up on behalf of the military.

## Abolition of the Military

In some countries there have been attempts to get rid of the army entirely as being a force which is beyond redemption. Success has been patchy.

*Costa Rica*   The most enduring experience has been in Costa Rica, a country, it must be added, where militarism never bit very deeply. In colonial times the country never attracted much attention from Spanish treasure seekers. There were no precious metals and few Indians to enslave so the Rich Coast did not have to endure the sorts of conquest, pillage and exploitation that places like Mexico and Peru underwent. Costa Rica had an agricultural economy with enough land for everyone, and property was not concentrated in the hands of a small number of landlords. In the nineteenth century liberal reforms came earlier than in many other Latin American countries. Nor was there a powerful and oppressive church to block reform. Free, obligatory, lay education, for instance, was decreed under the constitution of 1869.

After a brief civil war in 1948 between moderate conservatives and socialists, there was a national consensus that it would be a good thing to do away with the small army once and for all. This was duly done and to this day, even though the country is situated on a Central American isthmus which is riven with war and foreign intervention, Costa Rica subsists with only police forces. (That the Costa Rican National Guard was not quite as constabulary-minded as many Costa Ricans would like to think came home to me one day when I was visiting the School of the Americas, a military academy run by the United States and at that time operating at Fort Gulick in Panama. In one classroom I saw a Costa Rican National Guard officer attending a course on artillery. The Costa Rican police must be one of the few forces in the world to have expertise in field guns.)

*Bolivia* Less happy has been the experience of Melgarejo's homeland. Bolivia is at the far end of the spectrum from Costa Rica. Bursting with silver and other minerals and with a plentiful native population who could be made to exploit them, Upper Peru, as the country was known in colonial times, was a prime objective for Spain and its armies. Bolivia in the twentieth century is the poorest country in South America and deeply divided by wealth and race. In 1952 it nevertheless underwent one of the most radical revolutions experienced in South America, one in which organised labour and the peasants took on and defeated the small professional army. After a revolutionary regime under Víctor Paz Estenssoro took power, the army was all but abolished. But a few years later it was back. Lead by General René Barrientos it felt sufficiently strong to topple Paz in 1964 at the beginning of his third term of office. Within twenty years General García Meza was running the country for the drug barons.

The civilian politicians of Latin America seem fated to continue to co-exist and share power with the military. Latin America was born of a military imperialistic effort, Spanish America gained its independence from Spain by force of arms and the cult of militarism is too firmly rooted in the region's culture to be easily eradicated. In Brazil, Argentina, Peru and Chile, the military are overseeing the development of nuclear techniques. The Argentines and the Brazilians have rockets. What will happen when they get nuclear weapons?

# CHAPTER THREE

# THE GUERRILLAS

*The duty of every revolutionary is to make
revolution . . . it is not for revolutionaries to sit in the
doorways of their houses waiting for the corpse of
imperialism to pass by.*

FIDEL CASTRO

*You can never map out a strategy from A to Z. You must
have enough flexibility to change course, to accommodate the
line of action to changing historical circumstances, without
ever losing sight of the strategic objective. That is the
great lesson of the Frente Sandinista.*

COMANDANTE HENRY RUIZ OF THE FRENTE SANDINISTA DE LIBERACIÓN NACIONAL

―――――

It is a common misconception in the richer countries of the West in
general, and in Hollywood in particular, that Latin America is a
region peopled by many thousands of men, and not a few women,
who are professional guerrillas. Into town they ride every morning
from their jungle bivouacs to spread mayhem for some impossible
idealistic left-wing cause and when the sun goes down they ride off
again into the tropical dusk. Pancho Villa, the Mexican, was the
last man after all to presume to invade the United States: his
comrade-in-arms Emiliano Zapata died fighting for the heroic concept of 'Land and Liberty', Ernesto 'Ché' Guevara, the Argentine
doctor who fought with Fidel Castro in Cuba, went to a lonely
death in Bolivia.

While there are some guerrillas in Latin America who find self-
fulfilment only in that role, the majority are not like that. They are
offering armed resistance to established, but not necessarily legiti-

mate, governments. Elected governments who enjoy broad popular support being a rarity in Latin America, political legitimacy is uncommon. Men therefore take up arms not because they enjoy an adventurous open-air life but because they see it as the only way to overthrow those governments and supersede them. They may or may not be romantic, they are, like their civilian political counterparts, often riven by factionalism and are often unsuccessful, but they do have serious political intents. These intents usually have more to do with nationalism and democracy than, as some conservatives would have us believe, the furtherance of Soviet foreign policy aims.

For a guerrilla movement to be successful it must fulfil two requisites. Firstly its members must bear a coherent political message which they can communicate to a mass of people and persuade them to sympathise with. 'Guerrilla war,' said Ché Guevara, 'is a struggle of the masses, is a struggle of the people, the guerrilla group as the armed nucleus, is the fighting vanguard of it, its great strength is rooted in the mass of the population; the guerrilla then counts on all the support of the population of the place, that is a sine qua non.' Secondly it must have the moral and material resources to withstand the hostility of the regime it seeks to displace. 'The essential for the guerrilla,' said Guevara succinctly, 'shall be not to allow himself to be destroyed.' Only the most determined groups are able to fulfil those requisites.

Though the task of guerrilla groups in taking power is strewn with difficulties and sacrifices, these are as nothing compared with the task they face in wielding power when they win it. The skills needed for a successful military effort are not the same as those needed for the administration of an economy. The assertion of nationalism or anything that smacks of socialism or communism irritates the United States. In the case of Nicaragua now and Cuba, Bolivia, El Salvador and Guatemala in the most recent past, it has brought violent response, making the job of governing even more complicated and dangerous than it would otherwise have been for those who attain power.

Latin America has seldom seen the sort of set-piece battles between established armies that the rest of the world has been used to for centuries. The region was conquered for Spain and Portugal by mere handfuls of men. Columbus had a crew of no more than 90 for the three little ships with which he discovered America in 1492. Hernán Cortés overthrew the Aztec empire in what is now Mexico in 1519 with 700 soldiers and sailors, seventeen horses and ten cannon. Francisco Pizarro conquered the Incas in 1532 with an expedition numbering 180 men and 27 horses. Pedro de Valdivia started the long conquest of what is now Chile in 1540 with 150 Spaniards.

Guerrillas played a useful part in the overthrow of Spanish rule in the region at the beginning of the nineteenth century. The formal armies raised by the insurgent generals were aided time and time again by hordes of irregulars who harried the Spaniards in much the same way as Spanish irregular forces had been harrying the French troops occupying Spain itself. In what was to become Venezuela there were the *llaneros*, the undisciplined horsemen of the *llanos* or plains, led by men like Páez; in Argentina there were the *montoneros* ('the rabble'); in Uruguay there were the Tupamaros, who took their name from the eighteenth-century Indian leader, Tupac Amaru. In Cuba, which remained under the rule of Madrid till 1898, the cry of revolt was taken up by groups of white and black Cubans, the *mambises*, described by one historian as 'ill-armed and half-starving, many armed only with machetes', who for ten years from 1868 waged a savage war against the Spaniards. Later in the nineteenth century the cause of Cuban nationalism and the *mambises* was adopted by the Cuban writer, poet, mystic and revolutionary organiser José Martí. He started politics young and was condemned to six years penal servitude by the Spanish authorities and put in chains before he was seventeen. From a political base in the United States where he spent most of the last fourteen years of his life, Martí pushed ahead with plans for a full-scale war with the Spaniards. He died in 1895 in the first attack his men mounted in a new war against the colonial power. This war was to end three years later with the final ejection of the Spaniards from the New World but not before the United States had declared hostilities against Spain and taken much of the glory for the defeat of the European power from the islanders who had been attacking for most of the previous three decades. The memory of all these early guerrillas was to be revived and venerated in the twentieth century and their example followed. A guerrilla group sprang up, for instance, in Argentina in 1968 and attempted to weld the incoherent doctrines of General Perón onto the historical memory of the first *montoneros*. The twentieth-century Tupamaros in Uruguay invoked the name of their eighteenth-century precursors. When the radical wing of the Chilean Communist Party decided to launch a guerrilla movement, it was named after Manuel Rodríguez, a nineteenth-century Chilean guerrilla. Wherever twentieth-century guerrilla movements sprang up – and they sprang up with varying degrees of success in a majority of the countries of the region – their members were conscious that they were part of a strong historical tradition.

When the United States took over the mantle of Spain as the dominant power in the hemisphere – as President Monroe had hinted it would do – so Washington's government became the new enemy for the guerrillas. The United States, which in the nineteenth century dreamt of establishing an empire in the western hemisphere which would rival that of the British in Africa, Asia and the Caribbean, sought to extend its influence. It thereby necessarily collided with Latin Americans' own national feelings. Washington, for instance, offered to buy Cuba from Spain in 1848. Majority sentiment in the United States, a country which took a pride in its own history of resistance to British colonialism, was, however, for the most part hostile to any overtly colonialistic ventures. The White House and the State Department were therefore obliged to advance their country's interest by less direct means. They formed alliances with those conservative local leaders who put more store by the material advantages that alliance with Washington might bring than by the demands of national feeling. Those leaders often had to be backed up with shows of force or by the dispatch of expeditions and garrisons.

## Augusto César Sandino

Such was the case in the country which mounted one of the first guerrilla challenges to the United States. In 1926 the US Marines, who had maintained a garrison in Nicaragua from 1912 to 1925 in order to keep a pro-US government in power, returned to Managua. During the first occupation Nicaraguan national feeling was not sufficiently strong for there to have been much resistance. In 1926 it was different. A young Nicaraguan who had worked his way up through Central America to the oilfields of Mexico, converted to spiritualism and freemasonry and met up with Mexican revolutionaries. He returned home burning with patriotism.

'In those days,' said Augusto César Sandino, 'I used to meet with a group of spiritualist friends, and we commented daily on the submission of our Latin American people to the hypocritical or forceful advances of the murderous Yankee empire. On one occasion I told my friends that if there were in Nicaragua a hundred men who loved their country as much as I, our nation would recover its sovereignty, threatened as it was by that same Yankee empire. My friends replied that there surely must be that many men in Nicaragua, but that the difficulty lay in identifying them.'

He was indeed not immediately able to find a hundred and had to settle for no more than 29. On 2 November 1926 his band joined the Liberal Party cause and fired their first shots against the local Conservative allies of the United States. The Liberal politicians told him not to be a nuisance. By Christmas his band had shrunk to six and most of his weapons and ammunition had been lost. Nevertheless with the cheerful aid of some girls from the local brothel at Prinzapolca, the Liberal headquarters on the Caribbean coast, he rescued some of the rifles and at the age of 31 restarted his campaign against the occupation of his country.

His first manifesto quivered with nationalist feeling. 'The last of my soldiers, who are the soldiers of the freedom of Nicaragua, may die,' it said, 'but beforehand more than a battalion of yours, fairhaired invader, will have bitten the dust of my fertile mountains.'

For months afterwards, from his jungle base at El Chipote he was a thorn in the side of the Marines and the local Guardia police force which they had formed, trained and commanded. At last the Marines decided to mount an operation which would finally do away with him and El Chipote. Eduardo Crawley, in his book *Dictators never die*, writes:

> Wave after wave of bombers began to pound the wooded slopes, while two heavily armed columns of Marines and Guardia marched into the area. Their advance was made excruciatingly slow by continuous, hit-and-run harassment by Sandino's forces. It seemed as if every bend in the road, every clump of trees, every nightfall hid an ambush party ready to riddle them with rifle and machine-gun fire, or bombard them with deadly packs of cowhide containing sticks of dynamite and rusty scrap metal. It took the invading party the better part of a month to get into a position

from which they could launch a final assault on the heights
of El Chipote.

For years Sandino held at bay the Marines and the Guardia, and his
exploits went round the world. For instance, when the Kuo-
mintang marched victoriously into Peking in 1928 one of their units
was the Sandino Division. The war in Nicaragua was one of terror
and counter-terror. Traitors to the cause of Sandino or those who
were too slow in contributing to his war chest were done to death
with great cruelty with the machete. The United States forces used
aerial bombardment. In the bomber raid on the town of Ocotal in
July 1927, said to be the first ever carried out in the hemisphere,
Sandino lost 200 men and many civilians were killed.

But all the while that he was waging, and suffering, a war to the
death with the Marines, the guiding principles of his personal life
were those of mystic spiritualism. In 1930, he wrote to Colonel
Rivera, one of his commanders:

> Keep in mind that the divine law we are subject to is only
> one: the law of love. From that law of love all others derive.
> The law of love only recognises justice, its favourite
> daughter, born from its womb . . .
>
> Injustice comes from ignorance of the divine law, from
> the time that mankind was still in embryo form. Therefore,
> there is no reason for injustice, because it is against the law
> of love, the only one which will reign on Earth, when
> human fraternity finally prevails and man becomes light, as
> the Father, the Creator has ordained.

In 1933 Washington pulled out leaving the Guardia under Nicaraguan command for the first time, the command of a young man
who had ingratiated himself as an interpreter with the US Marines,
Anastasio 'Tacho' Somoza. Sandino was treacherously murdered
on 21 February 1934 by Somoza's Guardia. But in his own country
he was already a legend. Forgotten by all but the Nicaraguans, his
example lay dormant for decades. When it revived it was to prove
extraordinarily potent.

## Fidel Castro

While the spirit of Sandino lay dormant in Nicaragua Martí and the
*mambises* provided inspiration for a small group of nationalists in
Cuba. Moved by the same repugnance towards a corrupt govern-

ment and its close relation to the United States which Sandino had experienced in Nicaragua, Fidel Castro took up arms against the regime of Fulgencio Batista. Despite Castro's later claims that he had 'always been a communist', the historical record produces no evidence that he was familiar with or converted to Marxism–Leninism at this stage. His political vehicle was the M-26 or July 26th Movement, formed round a group of comrades who had been with him in his earliest protest actions against the Batista dictatorship.

In Batista, Castro was fighting the United States. As Castro was later to say of his country's relations with the United States, 'In economic and political matters relations have been solely unilateral . . . one party (the US) has decided our political principles and solved economic problems for us.' Batista had run Cuba from 1933 to 1940 through the medium of seven successive puppet presidents and had again seized power in a coup against an elected government in 1952. Despite that and the gangster measures which he used to stay in power, he was seen to be an ally of the United States. Between 1953 and 1958 he received $12 millionsworth of military aid from the United States and Washington maintained a large military mission in Havana.

On 25 November 1956, 82 men under Castro's leadership crammed into a motor launch, the *Granma*, and sailed from the Mexican port of Tuxpan for the eastern cost of Cuba. Ché Guevara described the scene:

> . . . the whole boat took on a ridiculously tragic appearance: men with anguished faces holding their stomachs, some with their heads in buckets, and others lying immobile on the deck, in the strangest positions, with their clothing soiled by vomit. With the exception of two or three sailors, and four or five others, the rest of the eighty-two crew members were seasick. But after the fourth or fifth day the panorama improved a bit. We discovered that what we thought was a leak in the boat was actually an open tap. We had already thrown overboard everything unnecessary in order to lighten the boat.

Ten days out from Tuxpan they landed on Cuban soil and the next day faced their first battle against Batista's men. All but fifteen were killed, but such was the detestation of Batista in Cuba and the popularity of their cause that they were in power in Havana in two years, having fought their way up the length of the long island.

When Castro had the reins of government in his hands he was not predisposed to accept guidance from a country such as the United States whose leaders were regarded by the Cubans as having cheated them of their victory over Spain, kept Cuba as a virtual protectorate and sided with an unpopular tyrant. The break between the guerrillas and the United States was not long in coming. On 17 March 1960 President Eisenhower gave the Central Intelligence Agency orders to prepare an exile army to invade the island. Three months later Castro took over the Western oil refineries on the island in retaliation for their unwillingness to process the Russian crude oil the government had bought. A week after that the United States government drastically cut the quota of high-priced sugar, the island's principal export, which the Cubans were permitted to sell in the US market. Three days later the Soviets announced they were willing to take the sugar. From then on the relationship went downhill fast. In April 1961 the US-backed Bay of Pigs invasion was staged and repulsed by the Cubans, by now armed with Soviet weapons. The following year the superpowers came into confrontation over the Soviets' action in stationing nuclear missiles on the island. The world came to the brink of a third world war because of the antipathy between a guerrilla government and a regional power. The guerrilla government, having rejected the apron strings of its former masters, found itself perforce under the physical and economic protection of another foreign power, the Soviet Union, which assured it against invasion and safeguarded its standard of living with very large cash subsidies. Despite this Castro himself remained a rebel, a man who saw the world in terms of a struggle between the rich northern half of the globe and the poor south rather than in terms of the East–West conflict which preoccupied Moscow. Within this vision and the inner conviction that he personally should take some strategic role in it, Castro maintained a degree of autonomy from the Soviet Union which was startlingly bold given the extent of Cuba's physical dependence. Castro has remained a nonconformist to the last. His actions were to prove an inspiration to those in Nicaragua who intended to revive the spirit of Sandino.

## The Sandinistas

After Sandino's murder Somoza and his two sons, Luis and Anastasio Junior ('Tachito'), went on to create a family dynasty which controlled Nicaragua until 1979. The family's landholdings represented about half the registered land in Nicaragua and a quarter of the best arable soil. No major businesses could survive without the Somozas' patronage and that patronage often involved the family taking a shareholding. An inventory of the family's shareholdings in the mid-1970s included 346 companies which ranged from the national airline, textiles and a travel agency to the manufacture of matches, distilleries and the exporting of human blood.

The first Anastasio Somoza was assassinated in 1956 and was succeeded by his elder son Luis, but it took till 1979 fully to avenge Sandino's murder. Three young men, Carlos Fonseca Amador, Silvio Mayorga and Tomás Borge, met in Tegucigalpa, the capital of Honduras, in July 1961 and decided to found a movement which would put an end to the Somoza dynastic dictatorship in the way that Fidel Castro had put an end to Batista two and a half years previously. They called it the Frente Sandinista de Liberación Nacional or the Sandinista Front for National Liberation. The FSLN was, like the man after whom it was named, not ideologically narrow. Fonseca always believed that the revolution against Somoza and in favour of a juster distribution of wealth could never succeed unless it had the broadest political base. 'I believe,' he wrote, 'the Nicaraguan revolutionary should embrace a doctrine which can lead the Nicaraguan people victoriously to liberation. In my own thought, I welcome the popular substance of different ideologies: Marxism, Liberalism and Christian Socialism.'

It took the three another two years to get together sixty men to mount the first military operation and among the fighters was one veteran, Santos López, who had himself fought with Sandino. It was not a success and the little group, based on the banks of the Coco River on the Nicaraguan–Honduran border, went through all sorts of privations. Borge, later to become the interior minister in the Sandinista government, later recalled, 'There was nothing to eat, not even animals to hunt. There was no salt. It wasn't just hunger that was terrible, but constant cold 24 hours a day, because we spent all our time in the river. We were always wet through with the clinging rain of that part of the country, the cold a kind of unrelieved torture, mosquitoes, wild jungle animals and insects. No shelter, no change of clothes, no food.'

85

It took them another decade and much loss of life in battles with Somoza's Guardia to achieve fame. In 1974 led by Germán Pomares, a former Conservative militant turned Sandinista, they pulled off an operation of great daring, seizing the guests at a Christmas party in the house of the Minister of Agriculture. The captives included General Pinochet's ambassador to Nicaragua, the Foreign Minister and Somoza's ambassador to the United States. The hostages were released only on the freeing of a number of political prisoners (including Daniel Ortega, who was later to become president of Nicaragua), the payment of $2 million in ransom and the publication of a long guerrilla communiqué on radio and television and in the newspapers. The Sandinistas with 18 hostages were flown out to Cuba having also obtained a general wage rise for Nicaraguan workers and the Guardia soldiers.

In the mid-1970s, and especially after the death in battle of Fonseca in November 1976, there were serious splits in the ranks of the FSLN. The so-called Proletarian Tendency was strongly Marxist–Leninist, had its strength in Managua and rejected the idea of pulling all classes into the struggle for the future of Nicaragua, while the GPP or Prolonged People's War was stronger in the countryside and predicted that the dictatorship would be overthrown only after working-class Nicaraguans had thoroughly imbibed Marxism–Leninism. The third tendency, the one which was perhaps nearest to the spirit of Sandino and Fonseca themselves and was finally to become dominant, preached the strategy of forming the widest possible alliance of classes in order to overthrow the Somozas. Unity was, as Castro urgently suggested and the traditions of the movement demanded, finally reforged. The FSLN rapidly gained strength as the maddened Somoza struck blindly at civilians. By mid-1979 the Sandinistas had, with great popular support and much to their surprise, defeated the Guardia. The Carter administration was nervous of the Sandinistas. When it was clear that Tachito could hold out no longer, Washington tried its best to maintain some sort of status quo by attempting to persuade the triumphant Sandinistas to retain the Guardia. To no avail. Tachito was put to flight on 17 July and a year or so later killed with a bazooka in a street in Asunción, the capital of Paraguay, probably by a group of Argentine guerrillas. A failed guerrilla leader of the 1930s had, by his ideas and actions, inspired a guerrilla movement in the 1970s which was able to take power.

Like their comrades and mentors in Cuba, however, the Sandinistas had little for which to thank Washington. The United States administration secretly moved against the victorious guerrillas almost as soon as they took over; and when Ronald Reagan succeeded Jimmy Carter there was no doubting that they had a formidable enemy in the White House.

A further complication set in when the economy began to go wrong. Neither in Havana nor in Managua did the guerrillas come into power with well-prepared plans for the economy beyond the grand general objective of redistributing income for the benefit of the poorest. Unfamiliarity with government combined with ambitious projects for changing society would, in the best of circumstances, have been a recipe for difficulty. The changes in society, which by definition upset the interests of the pro-United States supporters of the ancien régime, increased United States disfavour.

In 1983 the Reagan administration banned trade with Nicaragua, a very severe blow to the Sandinistas. This recipe for economic chaos was compounded in Cuba and Nicaragua by the fact that, as conditions worsened under the pressure of the government's own mistakes and hostility from the United States, skilled middle-class professionals in all walks of life began to emigrate. The guerrillas turned administrators were able to blame Washington for their economic difficulties: the United States government was able to point to the inability of the guerrillas to manage their own affairs. A more devilish set of vicious circles would be difficult to imagine.

Relations between the Nicaraguan government and the United States were exacerbated by the campaign waged by right-wing émigrés in the United States. This campaign was all the more effective in that the émigrés had the successful experience and advice of the Cuban lobby to follow. Repeating in the 1980s the mistakes they had committed in their dealings with Castro in the early 1960s, United States officials aided the émigrés to mount military operations against the government in Managua. At first this was done secretly; later, when secrecy was no longer possible, it was claimed they were acting in the interests of US national security. The Sandinistas found little effective military support from Western Europe. The governments there were unwilling to compromise their relations with the United States for the sake of the inexperienced guerrilla administration of a small Central

American country. When the Contra campaign became serious, the Sandinistas had little alternative but to seek aid from the Cubans and the Soviets. This in its turn was grist to the mill of those conservatives in the United States who argued that the Sandinistas had always been communists and that there was no alternative to aiding the supporters of the old Somoza regime.

## 'Ché' Guevara

The majority of guerrilla movements do not achieve power as Castro and the Sandinistas have achieved power. Latin America is littered with the graves of insurgent movements which flourished briefly and then died under the weight of military repression or their own inability to build a lasting popular base, or both.

The most instructive case of guerrilla failure is that of Ernesto Guevara, the close companion of Castro who was captured and killed in Bolivia in 1967 and who has gone down in history under the name of 'Ché', the term of endearment which Argentines use among themselves. Ernesto was born on 14 June 1928 in Rosario, Argentina, to reasonably prosperous parents. He qualified as a doctor in 1953 but since his adolescence he had been passionately committed to politics. He embraced Marxism–Leninism long before Castro did and was a committed communist from 1954 when an elective, reformist government in Guatemala was overthrown in a right-wing military coup encouraged by the United States. He was, as we have seen, aboard the *Granma* and fought his way with Castro to the final victory in January 1959. He was made a Cuban citizen a month later. For months he was left in command of the fortress of La Cabaña which dominates the Cuban capital. His closeness to the Cuban leader weighed more than his Argentine origins. He was named president of the National Bank of Cuba and his signature – a plain 'Ché' – appeared on Cuban banknotes. He was named Minister of Industries and tried – unsuccessfully – to diversify the country's economy away from sugar, its principal export.

In the years after Castro's victory – and with a good deal more rigorous Leninist ideological theory than Castro – Guevara set himself the task of planning a universal revolutionary strategy which would draw on the lessons he believed had been taught by the Cuban experience. That experience which had ended with the installation of a Marxist–Leninist government – albeit of a highly idiosyncratic character which owed almost all to the immense will-power of Castro himself – had started from the military action of a dozen people, few of whom accepted Marxism–Leninism as their intellectual guide.

In a study first published in the month of the guerrillas' triumphal entry into Havana, Guevara argued a triple thesis: that an irregular armed band can win against a regular army, that a centre of armed revolutionary activism, a *foco*, can advance the onset of revolution even when what the orthodox Leninist would call 'the objective conditions' do not exist and that favourable terrain for the armed struggle can be found in the countryside – in contradiction to the orthodox communist thesis that the fount of revolution is the oppressed urban proletariat led by a Marxist–Leninist 'vanguard' party. The thesis was called *foquismo* and was a frontal challenge to the communist establishment in Latin America and the rest of the world. *Foquismo* was not popular with those old Latin American communists who had in their tiny, unpopular, city-based vanguard parties laboured with little success to keep the flame of Marxism–Leninism alive. On an entirely personal level it was understandable that they objected to the Castroites, few of whom had been Marxist–Leninists a decade before, making free with the holy writs of their world movement. For the Soviets there was an added difficulty as, at the same time as the Cuban leader was impudently arguing that the Russians were making Marxism into a 'religious doctrine with its Rome, its Pope and its Ecumenical Council', Havana was arguing that Moscow should not only defend the island but subsidise it with hard currency that the Soviets could ill afford.

*Foquismo* however was not a concept that would disappear. With *foquismo* Guevara forged the link between the historical Latin American tradition of the guerrilla and the thought of Marx and Lenin. This link was further elaborated in the works of Régis Debray, a young French intellectual who had studied in Paris with the Marxist philosopher Louis Althusser and had gone to Cuba in 1961. In 1966 he was appointed to the chair of philosophy at the University of Havana and was later captured and imprisoned in Bolivia while on a mission to Guevara's guerrillas.

In 1955 Debray wrote,

The Cuban revolution has established that in the insur-rectional phase of the revolution, while it is indispensable to have some sort of organisation and firm political leadership (July 26th Movement), it is possible to do without a vanguard Marxist–Leninist party of the working class. It should be emphasised that this applies only to the preparatory stage of the seizure of power, for the creation of such a party becomes indispensable in the construction of a socialist society.

The joining of the guerrilla tradition to the Marxist–Leninist tradition was not, for Guevara personally at least, to be a successful enterprise. But in the first years after the guerrillas' victory in Cuba, the island was being counter-attacked from the United States and with Washington's encouragement shunned by its Latin American neighbours. In 1962 Cuba was excluded from the Organisation of American States and was therefore desperate for some friendly revolutionary ally in the western hemisphere. Castro felt that the fomenting of revolution in the region was a good way of moving world attention away from Cuba and at the same time satisfying his own conviction that he himself could play a major role in continent-wide, perhaps world-wide, armed revolution.

In April 1965 Guevara disappeared from Havana and for eight months travelled the world visiting revolutionary situations. By the end of the year he was back in Cuba taking part in the organisation of the Tricontinental conference which was to bring together the left from all over the Third World and making plans for his own most ambitious revolutionary stroke of all. With Cuban help and a group of Cuban and Bolivian fighters he would install a guerrilla movement in Bolivia, the landlocked geographic heart of South America, from whence the tides of revolution would lap outwards till the region was enveloped by the forces of change. Bolivia itself was at the time ruled by an air force general, René Barrientos, who attempted to pass himself off as a defender of the rights of the common people but who was little more than the latest in the long series of opportunistic military rulers in the mould of Melgarejo. By November 1966 local preparations in Bolivia were advanced and Ché and 16 experienced Cubans arrived in La Paz to begin the continental revolution. Within a year the operation had ended in total catastrophe.

Even as the newcomers arrived, the portents were not good. The Bolivian Communist Party was doubtful about the whole enterprise but if it was to go ahead its leader, Mario Monje, was insistent that it should come under his command. He understandably did not want an attempt at revolution being carried out in his country by a group of foreigners. The difficulties were papered over and the group travelled to the remote south-east of Bolivia where with 30 Bolivians they set up their principal encampment at Ñancahuazú. This was a 1227-hectare farm in a remote and lightly populated ranching area 225 kilometres from the nearest big city, Santa Cruz.

The choice could hardly have been worse. The remoteness of the area and the lack of connection of all sorts, physical, racial, cultural, economic, linguistic, meant that Ñancahuazú was to all intents and purposes not in Bolivia at all. The peasantry had little contact, or indeed knowledge, of the politics of La Paz and its ruler. The region was more prosperous than many in Bolivia and if life there was not easy it was not of the grinding poverty of the mining areas of the high Andes where a tin miner could expect to contract pneumoconiosis in the horrifically unsafe mines and be useless for work by the time he was in his mid-thirties. But Guevara's band could not have lit the torch of revolt among even the most radical local inhabitants. The local language was Guaraní and none of Guevara's band, not even the Bolivian members, could speak it. Moreover there was in this remote area of semi-wilderness neither the feeling of bruised nationalism nor the folk-memory of earlier guerrilla exploits so central to the Nicaraguan and Cuban struggles. The factor of nationalism was, if anything, working against the guerrilla group whose nucleus was Cuban and who were being led by a native Argentine. General Gary Prado, who as a young captain commanded the infantry company responsible for the capture of Guevara, was later to argue that when the guerrillas came out in the open the fact that they were foreigners prevented open support from the political organisations of the left. Ché Guevara and his band were unable to pass their revolutionary message to the peasants in the area in which they were operating and make them understand it: their political relations with their urban supporters were far from satisfactory either.

Nor were they able to withstand the counter-attacks of the Bolivian army which had been the object of special counter-insurgency training by the United States. When a group of particularly determined revolutionaries came to power in Bolivia in 1952 under President Víctor Paz Estenssoro, they had all but done away with the army. But within six years the politicians in La Paz were in need of it to face the even more determined and radical armed miners and the army was built up again with US help. It was rebuilt so well that in 1964 senior officers, including Barrientos, were able to cut short Paz' second presidency and send him into exile. By 1967 the army had recovered its traditional power and political influence.

Washington had good intelligence about the guerrillas' strategy and a firm resolve to destroy them. When the presence of a guerrilla force was confirmed Washington was swift to move. By April 1967 the United States army had set up a camp for training the Bolivian army in counter-insurgency at a disused sugarmill at La Esperanza, 80 kilometres north of Santa Cruz. There a 'Mobile Training Team', commanded by Mayor Ralph W. 'Pappy' Shelton, got down to the job of training a special force of the Manchego regiment in the techniques of fighting guerrillas. In August the training operation was important enough to be visited by the most senior officer of the United States forces in Latin America, General Robert Porter, Commander-in-Chief of US Southern Command based in Panama.

The training was good and rapid and in a very short time the balance of initiative tilted against Guevara's men. Their supply lines with supporters in the cities were badly co-ordinated. Nor was the area of operations an agricultural zone off whose produce Guevara's men could live. There was plenty of cattle ranching but precious few fields under crops. And they were left without essentials including medicine. In his writings on guerrilla warfare Guevara had remarked, 'The guerrilla needs an iron constitution which allows him to resist all adversity without getting ill and to transform his existence as a hunted animal into another factor which strengthens him.' In the event he himself was an asthmatic. His disability often left him physically prostrate though, as Prado recalls, his hold over the members of the guerrilla band was such that his authority was never questioned.

In April moreover, Guevara made a major tactical error in splitting his tiny force into two groups. Those two groups wandered round looking for each other and were never able to reunite. After a number of small battles in which the guerrillas lost men and the army gained increasing intelligence about them, the group commanded by Guevara was cornered by a company of the army under Prado in a small scrubby gulch, the Quebrada del Churo which leads down to the Río Grande, not far from the village of La Higuera. At about one o'clock in the afternoon of 7 October 'Willy' Simón Cubas (a Bolivian miner) and Ché Guevara were captured. Prado had them marched to La Higuera and there lodged in separate rooms in the schoolhouse overnight as he awaited further orders.

After dinner, Prado recounts, he went over to check on the two prisoners interested in getting to know his prize captive, one of the most famous men in Latin America. He brought over a packet of Astoria cigarettes and a box of matches for Guevara. Guevara stuffed the tobacco from two cigarettes in the bowl of his pipe and began an evening's conversation with Prado on the reasons for his campaign. There was, as recounted by Prado, one particularly memorable exchange.

> 'Your ignorance, the backwardness in which they keep you here, doesn't allow you to understand what's going on in the continent . . . your liberation is on the way,' said Guevara.
>
> 'Look, comandante,' replied Prado, 'my family is from here, from this region, from Vallegrande, I grew up in these valleys, in these mountains, I had to walk two leagues from Guadalupe to Vallegrande to go to school, alongside the sons of peasants. I've met classmates here, my childhood friends, and all of them are ready to help us, to help the army; and those bonds are stronger than any ideas you might be able to bring in from outside.'
>
> 'You have to realise,' Guevara answered, 'that all we Latin Americans are in a struggle that is continent-wide and where there are, and will be many deaths, that will cost much blood, but the war against imperialism can't be stopped. It has its fronts here in Bolivia, in Colombia, in Venezuela and in Central America and you military men have to decide if you are with your people or in the service of imperialism.'

The following day, 9 October, orders having come from La Paz at about 11 a.m., the battalion commander Colonel Andrés Zenteno called for volunteers. Warrant Officer Mario Terán and Sergeant Bernardino Huanca stepped forward, took automatic rifles and entered the schoolrooms where the two prisoners were lying. Without a word spoken, according to Prado, the two were killed in a burst of gunfire.

At 1.45 the Bolivian army officially announced, 'El Ché Guevara ha muerto ayer en combate' – Ché Guevara died yesterday in combat. The most ambitious attempt to graft Latin American Marxism–Leninism onto the historical tradition of the Latin American guerrilla had failed.

The failure of Guevara has been the subject of a number of ideological autopsies. He was ill-advised in the choice of Ñancahuazú as the site of his *foco*, and the tactical management of his campaign was defective. But in the light of Castro's initial success against Batista and the subsequent success of the Sandinistas in taking power and maintaining themselves against every sort of pressure put on them by the United States, it is clear that Guevara fell down on two important counts. He was unable to tap the founts of nationalism or patriotism that moves a population against a readily visible enemy. And he was unable to subordinate his own political beliefs into a common political effort able to attract the co-operation of the very large sections of society needed to overthrow a dictatorship by force.

The circumstances surrounding the defeat and death of Guevara have faded from memory a little and the victory of the Sandinistas is in sharper focus in today's Latin America. The guerrilla tradition is still very much alive, even if the lessons of the Sandinistas and of Castro in his early days – the vital importance of preserving unity and of trying to appeal to the widest section of society – are not always observed. In 1986 one guerrilla group came within an ace of assassinating Augusto Pinochet, the dictator of Chile. In Guatemala three guerrilla groups are continuing a war which has been going on since Guevara was there in 1954. In El Salvador the tradition of Farabundo Martí is alive among the FMLN guerrillas who have been trying to seize power since 1979.

As long as the region suffers from governments that are unpopular and dictatorial, the guerrilla tradition will continue.

# CHAPTER FOUR

# THE CHURCH

*. . . it seems to us relevant to mention here what a priest
from the province of Quito told us, during his visitation of his
parish, in which – between feasts and memorial services for the
dead – he received each year over 200 sheep, 6000 poultry, 4000
Indian pigs, and 50000 eggs. Nor is his parish one of the more
lucrative ones . . .*

REPORT TO KING FERDINAND VI OF SPAIN BY NAVAL OFFICERS JUAN AND ULLOA, 1748

*The Catholic who is not a revolutionary is living in mortal sin*

FATHER CAMILO TORRES, COLOMBIAN GUERRILLA PRIEST, 1966

There cannot be many more elections in the Vatican City before a
Latin American is chosen as Pope. With 130 million inhabitants,
the bulk of them – notionally at least – Catholics, Brazil is the
world's largest Catholic country. And with Latin America making
an important contribution to the intellectual life of the Catholic
Church and to its administrative bureaucracy, it would be perverse
if this were not acknowledged.

The Church in Latin America has always had the character of its
colonisers, Spain and Portugal, stamped all over it. The physical
remains of that Spanish and Portuguese church are there to delight
the eye to this day. In the city centre of Santo Domingo, the first
European city founded in America, stands the cathedral of Santa
María, a beautiful little church built of white coraline stone. Work
was started on it by Diego, Columbus' son, as early as 1512.
Authorised by Pope Julius II, it is a building which owes as
much to the gothic styles of Europe as to the renaissance. The old
colonial heart of what was an inner-city slum beside the Caribbean

has recently been carefully restored with the help of the Spaniards and now the rich and fashionable have returned and reclaimed and beautified the houses. As you turn the corner of Isabel la Católica Street and come upon the gleaming cathedral in its little square in the hot sun, you have the delicious, exotic sensation of being in some sleepy little Andalusian town beside the Mediterranean. In the cool dark interior under the vaulting and the pointed arches is Columbus' tomb, a florid concoction of marble and wrought iron donated by the Spanish government at the end of the last century after the Discoverer's bones were found under the flagstones. On the high altar is an ancient picture of the Virgin carrying the Child Jesus, her crown supported by three angels, Ferdinand and Isabella kneeling at her feet. The cathedral has no tower. Philip II gave express orders that the planned tower should not be built lest some enemy capture it and overlook the city's fortifications.

Or there are the towns of Ouro Preto and Congonhas do Campo in the Brazilian state of Minas Gerais which poured gold and diamonds into the Portuguese treasury in the eighteenth century. They were once places of great wealth but are now abandoned to the tourists who come to see the sinuous lines of scores of mouldering rococo churches which could have been transported there from Bavaria. At Congonhas on the staircase which leads up to the church of Bom Jesús are the powerful stone statues of the prophets, Jonah, Job and the rest each carrying his biblical text, carved in 1800 by master sculptor António Francisco Lisboa – O Aleijadinho, The Little Cripple. There are few large towns in the region where the Church of colonial times, whatever its many other failings, has not left some monument of beauty.

This Church took root in the New World in 1492, the same year that Muslim power was finally broken in Western Europe. In the year Columbus stepped ashore in the Bahamas there ended in Granada a Christian crusade which had gone on for nearly eight centuries. In 711 a Muslim commander, Tarik, invaded Spain from North Africa and by 718 virtually the whole of the country was in Muslim hands. From that year Christian Spaniards and Portuguese were to devote themselves to counter-attack, to the uprooting of Islam as a political and religious force on their peninsula. It was an undertaking which demanded that the faith of the Church and the military resources of the Monarchy were of necessity intertwined. The process bound Church and State together as nowhere else in Europe.

In 1492 the last Muslim king of Granada was vanquished by Columbus' patrons Ferdinand and Isabella. With Columbus' discovery of America the prospects appeared of another crusade abroad at the precise moment that the one at home was completed. What could be more natural than that the Catholic sovereigns who had just claimed the last corner of Spain for Christ should take on the proud new responsibility of extending His, and their, kingdom to the New World?

Thus it was that Columbus, who had been reading the account of Marco Polo's travels as he sailed westward, arrived in what he believed to be the East Indies with a mandate from Ferdinand and Isabella to gain lands for the crown and help conquer souls for Christ.

No one in Europe at the time of Columbus' voyages or for years afterwards had the slightest doubt about the rights Spain and Portugal possessed to take control of the New World. Had not Pope Alexander VI decreed in 1493 that the Portuguese should control everything east of a line out in the Ocean and the Spaniards everything to the west of it? And was he not – in theory at least – the supreme arbiter among the world's rulers?

The story of the Church in Spanish America is hereafter the story of two sets of men. The majority broadly identified the interests of the faith with the interests of the establishment, as the Pope had done and as had been the case for centuries in Spain. The minority saw dangers in muddling what was Caesar's with what was God's.

## Church and State

The upholders of the establishment were in a powerful position. The Spanish crown had forged a strong link with the Church at home and virtually imposed its will on it. There was no question now of the civilian authorities being disposed to let the Church do what it wanted in the colonies. The popes acknowledged what they could not prevent and so the crown was able to appoint and dismiss bishops and fix their remuneration as it wanted, without awaiting permission from Rome. It set the boundaries of the diocese and allowed no church, monastery or hospital to be set up without its permission. No churchman travelled to the New World without official permission. Given that it controlled travel to and communication with America, the crown's hold on the Church in America was, if anything, stronger than it had been on the Church in Spain itself.

The colonists for their part brought over from Spain Santiago Matamoros, Saint James the Slayer of the Moors, as their patron, the saint who had so helped them in their reconquest of their own land from the infidel. They named churches, towns and provinces after him, Santiago de los Caballeros on Hispaniola, Santiago de Cuba, Santiago de Chile, Santiago del Estero, four towns called Matamoros in Mexico, Santiago de Veraguas in Panama, Santiago de María in El Salvador and on and on and on. Before long it was being rumoured that Santiago on horseback, sword in hand, was appearing on the side of the Spanish troops as they fought against the heathen and made the New World safe for exploitation by the empire.

For its part the Church through the inquisition maintained a discipline over the beliefs of its members, a process which had the additional effect of policing the empire against protestants and other heretics who would be tempted to deny the king's authority. In the manner of the Soviet KGB, the inquisitors sought out and imprisoned those who were suspected of being heterodox, turning proven heretics over to the civil power for execution. The inquisitors were on hand when ships docked to check on the beliefs of the passengers and the suitability of any reading matter which was carried in the cargo. The reading of novels was forbidden, as was the writing of them.

The demands of faith, the requirements the colonists had for labour and the interests of orderly government, the crown thought, could be dovetailed if the natives were put into the charge of a Spaniard. In exchange for his work the native would be instructed in the truths of the Catholic religion while the colonist kept an eye on him. The system was called the *encomienda* and the Spaniards who were given an *encomienda* and power over the natives were known as *encomenderos*. The stage was set for the development of mining businesses and plantations which were to make the settlers rich and the crown of Spain the most powerful in Europe while the indigenous peoples were reduced to effective slavery which millions are still suffering to this day.

It was not long, however, before the evangelical-minded minority clashed with the establishment-minded majority. As the first colonists took possession of the island of Hispaniola, today divided between Haïti and the Dominican Republic, they took possession of its inhabitants and reduced them to slavery. After all, they argued, it was not clear whether or not these creatures were indeed human kind and deserving of treatment as such.

A Dominican friar, Antonio de Montesinos, had no doubt that that sort of arrangement and all that it implied for the natives was not for him. On the Sunday before Christmas 1511, in the little thatched church at the Spanish settlement on Hispaniola, he launched his attack on the way the Europeans were treating the native Tainos who were dying by the hundreds of thousands and who within forty years were destined to disappear as a race completely. His words were the first recorded denunciation by the Church of slavery in America, and the first open declaration of the Church's role as an institution for all men, whatever their colour.

> This voice says that you are in mortal sin, that you live and die in it, for the cruelty and tyranny you use in dealing with these innocent people. Tell me, by what right or justice do you keep these Indians in such a cruel and horrible servitude? On what authority have you waged a detestable war against these people, who dwelt quietly and peacefully on their own land? . . . Why do you keep them so oppressed and weary, not giving them enough to eat, not taking care of them in their illness? For with the excessive work you demand of them they fall ill and die, or rather you kill them with your desire to extract and acquire gold every day. And what care do you take that they should be instructed in religion? . . . Are these not men? Have they not rational souls? Are you not bound to love them as you love yourselves?

Montesinos' words have echoed down the centuries among those Christians who felt that what the establishment ordered was not necessarily what Christian faith demanded. Montesinos got a telling off from the king when his words reached Spain three months later, and the Dominican superior in Hispaniola was ordered by his superior in Spain to stop such scandalous nonsense being aired by his friars. But his like could not be stopped. Bartolomé de las Casas, another Dominican friar who was eventually made a bishop, lobbied the crown endlessly on both sides of the Atlantic for the cause of the indigenes arguing, without much consistency, that it was better to import slaves from Africa than to let the natives succumb to the toll that the Spanish settlers put upon them.

The situation was much the same under the Portuguese crown in Brazil and again there were clergy willing to speak out against the effective slavery the native and blacks were living in. In a sermon at Epiphany 1662, the formidable Portuguese Jesuit Antônio Vieira thundered:

> Can there be a greater want of understanding, or a greater error of judgment between men as men, than for me to think that I must be your master because I was born further away from the sun, and that you must be my slave because you were born nearer to it?

In a Lenten sermon he declared:

> I know what you are going to tell me . . . our people, our country, our government cannot be sustained without Indians. Who will fetch a pail of water for us or carry a load of wood? Who will grind our manioc? Will our wives have to do it? Will our sons? . . . But when necessity and conscience require such a thing, I answer yes and repeat again yes. You, your wives, your sons, all of us are able to sustain ourselves with our own labour. It is better to live from your own sweat than from the blood of others!

In many parts of Latin America – and indeed many other places – those words are as relevant today as when Montesinos and Vieira pronounced them.

For more than a century after the Conquest, the Church in Latin America stayed more or less true to its evangelistic calling. In 1531 the Virgin appeared to a poor Mexican peasant on a little hill outside Mexico City and commanded him to have a church built there in her honour. It took much persuading for the bishop to allow it, but it was eventually built and became the most famous pilgrimage site in America. The image of the dark-skinned Virgin of Guadalupe is still revered there. The original church, now engulfed by the city, has given way to a much larger and uglier modern concrete construction where the faithful are borne past the image on its solid silver altar on a moving walkway.

The Dominicans, the Franciscans and the Jesuits pushed out into the interior of the continent, seeking to bring the word of God to the heathen. At the beginning of the seventeenth century in the centre of South America, in Paraguay and the surrounding area, the Jesuits started to build 'reductions'. These were mission stations with great churches and orderly towns for the lay people where the native peoples, mostly Guaranís, were organised in thriving communities where they spoke their own languages and had little to do with the settler population. By the middle of the eighteenth century there were 40 reductions with a population of perhaps 130 000.

The Guaranís were skilful craftsmen. The ruins of their buildings stand today amid rolling hills along the Paraná River with all the grandeur and majesty of a Fountains Abbey or a Rievaulx, their red sandstone surfaces covered with fine carving of a quality which would not be out of place in any European cathedral. At the reduction of Trinidad there is a particularly fine frieze which shows angels playing all sorts of musical instruments – one is at the organ while another mans the bellows, another plays the violin, a fourth a harp, a fifth a trumpet. The angels are rather flat-faced and clearly taken from local models.

In the workshops the Guaranís learnt to become blacksmiths, and bellfounders, gilders and calligraphers. 'We have trumpets and watches made here,' one Jesuit wrote, 'not inferior to those of Nuremberg and Augsburg.' In one of the Paraguayan reductions in the eighteenth century, a Jesuit astronomer set up a sophisticated observatory and corresponded with scientists from Peking to St Petersburg. The indigenes were certainly treated paternalistically by the missionaries and none of them appears ever to have been ordained priest. But, protected from the *bandeirantes*, the fierce Brazilian slave merchants, they lived a more peaceful and secure life than those who fell prey to the white entrepreneurs.

The first century of Christianity in Latin America produced a number of men and women who were so outstanding that Rome decided to declare them saints. Some, like Toribio de Mogrovejo, the second archbishop of Lima, were in positions of influence and authority. He had no hesitation in defying the king's viceroy in Lima when he thought it necessary and he pounded the deserts and jungles organising the church in his vast territory simply, modestly and tirelessly. Others were complete unknowns, like Martín de Porres, the bastard son of a black woman from Panama and a Spaniard who went on to become governor of Panama. He spent his life as a lay brother in the Dominican friary in Lima looking after the sick and devoting himself to a life of prayer. There were also remarkable women, Rose of Lima and Mariana of Quito, who led lives of mysticism behind convent walls.

At a time when the Church seemed moved by the fate of the indigenes but not too concerned about the black slaves imported from Africa, the record of Peter Claver, a Catalan-born Jesuit who lived in the port of Cartagena, now in Colombia, stands out. Cartagena and Vera Cruz in Mexico were the two ports licensed by the Spanish crown to receive African slaves, and rich men from all over the empire came to buy at their slave markets. The merchandise arrived in terrible condition off the ships, their legs in fetters, chained naked together in sixes, having been confined to a fetid hold with no sanitation and little food for weeks during the passage of the tropics. Born in 1580, Claver worked for forty years in Cartagena baptising and doing what he could to relieve the sufferings of the hundreds of thousands of unfortunate men, women and children who passed through the port. He often came up against the hostility of the slave owners and indeed of his own superiors who regarded him as morose and melancholic because of his preference for the company of blacks over that of whites. In his last feeble years before he died he was in the charge of a young black who took a delight in humiliating a man who could not feed or dress himself, forgetting to give him his food or eating the best bits of it himself. The room in which he died in 1654, probably of Parkinson's disease, is still to be seen today in Cartagena. At the time of his death it was full of flyblown garbage which no one would clear away.

The Church's best efforts were not however enough to instil a thorough orthodox knowledge of the Catholic religion into the whole population of Latin America. Shortage of missionaries and the very large distances to be covered, combined with the unwillingness of many indigenous peoples to give up all of their original beliefs, meant that millions ended up with a patchwork of dogmas stitched together from Christianity and from pre-Christian faiths. The situation was complicated by the fact that the millions of black slaves who were imported from Africa also brought their beliefs over to the New World.

By the eighteenth century the spiritual energies of the Church were waning and the Church was better characterised by the prosperous parish priest of Quito than by a Montesinos or a Martín de Porres. The contributions and the legacies of the faithful and the patronage of the State had transformed the Church into an institution of power and wealth and had dimmed its Christian message. This decline into the spiritual doldrums was intensified by the disappearance of the Jesuits. In 1759 the Portuguese king exiled them from his dominions and eight years later the Spanish king followed suit. A big new reduction, at Jesús in Paraguay, was left half-built. The date of 1767 can still be seen at the top of the last pillar to be erected in the church. When the Jesuits departed the Church lost hundreds of devoted and hardworking intellectuals. The order was later revived but not before immense harm had been done to the Church's standing.

When the colonies decided to cut free of Spain at the beginning of the nineteenth century, it was only to be expected that many Church leaders opted to try and defend the status quo and the privileges that association with the crown had given them. The more junior clergy, closer to the people, often saw the revolution against Spain as a positive development. Two leaders of the Mexicans' revolt against Spanish rule were priests.

Miguel Hidalgo, the turbulent parish priest of the small town of Dolores, was mixed up in the plotting against Spanish rule. Early in the morning of 16 September 1810, Hidalgo had the bells rung for mass specially early and urged his congregation to rise up under the banner of the Virgin of Guadalupe against unjust Spanish rule. For a few months he was able to lead a ragged army of thousands against the forces of Spain but by March the following year he was beaten and captured and turned over to the Inquisition. He was defrocked for heresy and treason and handed over to the civil government who cut his head off and displayed it on a pole, to frighten anyone tempted to follow his example. To this day on the anniversary the presidents of Mexico repeat the Grito de Dolores, Hidalgo's proclamation at Dolores.

His cause was not long in being taken up by another priest, José María Morelos, who fought a guerrilla war against the Spaniards till in 1815 he, too, was captured, defrocked and executed by firing squad. Though Church and State were to be bitterly at odds later in Mexican history, the first heroes of an independent Mexico were churchmen whose actions Montesinos would surely have approved of.

The nineteenth century in general was a wretched time for the Church in Latin America as highly conservative popes in Rome called for an offensive against the forces of liberalism which, in Latin America as in Europe, were reacting to the wealth and privilege which the Church had accumulated over the centuries. The Church, for its part, was unwilling to give up the material riches and the political control that it had enjoyed under the colonial regime. In some countries, notably Brazil, Chile, Cuba and Uruguay, the Church was disestablished. In others, such as Argentina, Colombia and Peru, the old Church–Government axis of colonial times was more or less retained. Nowhere did the Church keep a stronger hold than in Ecuador, which had been a very important religious centre in colonial times. After independence from Spain all teaching, primary, secondary and university, was put in the hands of the Church and the preaching of other religions was forbidden. Gabriel García Moreno, a president who was something of a religious maniac, brought in a constitution in 1869 in which being a practising Catholic was a necessary condition of being an Ecuadorean citizen.

The first decades of the twentieth century were little better than the nineteenth, not least because much of the Church instinctively sided with Franco in the Spanish Civil War and with the Salazar dictatorship in Portugal. In Mexico, from 1926 onward, amid great bitterness the Church was actively persecuted and fanatical supporters of the Church's old position, the Cristeros or followers of Christ the King, rose in bloody revolt against the government. On 31 July 1926 the archbishop of Mexico City decreed an interdict – the Church went on protest strike for three years. For the first time in four centuries, in a country whose inhabitants still remained strongly Catholic, no masses were said, babies were left unbaptised, marriages were not solemnised and the dying were refused the last rites. One of the Cristeros, who had received counselling from a nun, assassinated President Alvaro Obregón in 1928 with five bullets in the head. The Cristeros were bloodily suppressed and there was bitterness between Church and State for years after. As late as 1986 the archbishop of Chihuahua threatened to impose an interdict in his diocese as a protest against electoral irregularity by the government, though he was finally dissuaded from going that far by the Vatican. (One of the incidental developments from the Church–State conflict in Mexico was that it brought a young newspaper reporter, Graham Greene, to Latin America for the first time in the 1930s and inspired him to write *The Lawless Roads* and *The Power and the Glory*.)

Sometime towards the middle of the twentieth century, the Vatican and the Church in Latin America woke up. They sensed that a traditionally Catholic region was about to slip away from them as many local Church leaders remained preoccupied by old battles, wedded to conservative doctrines. The leaders were unconscious of the new political and social strains racking a continent whose population was growing rapidly and where poverty was growing more and more widespread. Nor was there the personnel to tackle the problems, had they been diagnosed. From Rome Pius XII put out a call for priests from abroad to go urgently to help the native Latin American clergy with their task. At the same time efforts were made to modernise what structures remained. The number of priests at work went up from 24000 in 1945 to 38000 fifteen years later. In 1960 there were 7300 priests in Latin America who had been born in Spain, 1500 from Germany and more than 1100 from the United States. Even with the new influx the region was badly off compared to other parts of the Catholic world, with about two priests for every 10000 Catholics compared to more than twelve in Western Europe, and was very much worse off than in colonial times. In 1750 there had been 770 priests, one for every 779 Chileans: in 1810 in Mexico there had been more than 7400 priests for just over 6 million inhabitants.

At the end of the sixteenth century there had been just 31 dioceses in Latin America; by 1900 there were 69. In 1960 there were 456. Between 1956 and 1962, 70 new dioceses were set up in Brazil alone. The structure nevertheless remained precarious.

In any event the Church had never suffered such a shake-up, such an infusion of new blood and of the new ideas that the foreigners brought with them. Moreover the shake-up in the region was happening on the eve of a gigantic shake-up in the Church as a whole as, in 1959, John XXIII launched the Second Vatican Council. The Council and John's own writings established that the Church should once more concentrate its attention on the poor. As far as the Latin Americans were concerned it could only mean the wholesale dumping of the attitudes of two centuries which had seen bishops supporting the status quo and blessing the rule of any dictator, however repulsive, as long as he protected the material possessions and the civic dignity of the Church. It meant a return to the spirit of Montesinos.

Some had already anticipated the changes that were in the wind. A Spanish-born priest, Padre Sardiñas, had attached himself to Castro's guerrillas as they fought Batista in the mountains. A figure who trod a similar path but who, because of his social status and intellectual powers, was destined to become more famous, was the Colombian priest, Camilo Torres. Born of a rich professional family in Bogota in 1929 and taken to Europe to live for three years, Torres had a privileged upbringing with a private tutor. Despite being sickly he was a brilliant student and was lecturing at the university when he was seventeen. After a girlfriend of his became a nun, he decided to join the Dominicans. He was ordained priest and studied sociology at Louvain, returning to his native city to become a very popular university chaplain. In Bogota he entered fully into politics and moved quickly to the left.

In the face of the extreme conservatism of the Church, Torres rapidly came into collision with his superiors. In 1965, for instance, he delivered a speech in Bogota in which he proclaimed, 'The economic, military, ecclesiastical and political powers will wage war with the people in the face of the revolution which is approaching . . .'

After several requests to the Cardinal of Bogota he was laicised in June 1965. Later that year he joined the guerrillas of the ELN or Army of National Liberation in the field as an ordinary fighter. The ELN, which had nothing to do with the orthodox Colombian Communist Party and looked to the example of Fidel Castro, had only been in action a few months. On 15 February 1966, Torres' patrol ambushed a military detachment killing four. The army counterattacked and Torres was killed and buried in an unmarked grave.

The leader of the ELN, Fabio Vázquez, said of him after he died, 'He united the scientific concept of revolutionary war, considering it the only effective way to develop the fight for freedom, with a profound Christianity, which he extended and practised as a limitless love for the poor, the exploited and the oppressed.' The cardinal didn't see it like that.

## Liberation theology

The moves at the Second Vatican Council in Rome were meanwhile followed by two big regional Church conferences, each attended by the pope of the day, in Medellín, Colombia, in 1968 and in Puebla, Mexico, eleven years later, at which ways to apply the new teaching of the Church to the Latin American situation were discussed. These meetings gave the signal for the Latin American Church to declare its independence of the intellectual moulds in which the Europeans had up till now formed the theology of the Church worldwide. Frei Betto, a Brazilian Dominican who had been arrested and tortured by the military for his connections with opposition groups, argued that the European experience of two world wars and nazism had led European theologians to pose questions and argue about the value of the human being and the purpose of life. The Latin American situation, on the other hand, was dominated by the existence of millions of hungry people. It was one in which, according to United Nations figures, 40 per cent of the population, or 113 million people, were living in poverty and a half of those in utter poverty. To understand the forces which brought about that situation, Betto said, it was necessary to have recourse to the social sciences, including Marxism. 'To fear Marxism is like fearing mathematics because you suspect it was influenced by Pythagoras,' Betto said.

Out of such attitudes were born the ideas of the liberation theologians, whose work has affected Church attitudes worldwide and perturbed many, including John Paul II and much of the Latin American establishment.

The roots of liberation theology were well explained by one of its greatest exponents, the Brazilian Leonardo Boff, who was later summoned to Rome, interrogated about his beliefs and condemned to one year's silence. At the time of Puebla he said, 'Liberation theology is born out of ethical indignation, before the poverty and marginalisation of the great majority of people on our continent. This theology can't be understood without the spirituality which is moved in the presence of the poor man and sees in the poor man the suffering face of Christ.'

The new radicalism was not confined to theologians. Speaking in Paris in 1968 Helder Câmara, Archbishop of Olinda and Recife, one of the most squalid parts of Brazil, announced, 'I respect those who feel obliged in conscience to opt for violence – not the all too easy violence of armchair guerrillas, but those who have proved their sincerity by the sacrifice of their life. In my opinion, the memory of Camilo Torres and of Ché Guevara merits as much respect as that of Martin Luther King.'

In 1973 a group of six bishops in the Centre-West of Brazil

expressed themselves trenchantly in a pastoral letter to their flocks, 'It is necessary to overcome capitalism: the greater evil, accumulated sin, the rotten branch, the tree which produces those fruits which we know; poverty, hunger, sickness, death. . . .'

The break with what had come in earlier days to be accepted as doctrinal orthodoxy has been accompanied by breaks with the accepted organisation and practice of the Church. The formal structures of the Church, particularly the parish, have in many places been superseded by 'basic Christian communities', groups of friends who come together to worship – with a priest if they can find one, if not with a lay 'minister of the Word'. In the absence of enough priests, the Church has been obliged to delegate more and more duties to the laity.

In October 1987 I attended a mass at the house of a group of priests in Managua. It was said not in a chapel but in the patio of the house on a warm night under the stars in the company of a dozen of their friends. The furnishings on the table were minimal and the chalice, instead of being the sacred gold-lined vessel that canon law had for centuries demanded, was no more than an earthenware cup. The sermon was a reflection on the events of the week – the latest casualties in the war against the terrorists, the scarcities and so on – in which everyone joined. The atmosphere was very far removed from that of, say, the formal consecration of the cathedral in Santo Domingo but was certainly closer to that of the Last Supper.

Not all parts of the Church in Latin America were equally affected by these winds of change. Particularly in those countries where the Church and State had kept their links in the nineteenth century, there was a resistance to new ideas. Argentina became a prime example. In the decade of military rule which followed the overthrow of the government of Isabel Perón in 1976 and which was characterised by the forces' 'dirty war' against the opposition, only a tiny minority of the bishops condemned the kidnapping, torture, summary execution and other barbarities which they knew to be very widespread. One bishop who did speak out against the atrocities died in suspicious circumstances in a road accident. Even when one of their own number had most probably been killed by the military regime, the Argentine Church made no protest. The military said they were fighting for the preservation of 'Western Christian civilisation' and that seemed to be enough to satisfy the conservative majority. The Argentine Church, almost to a man, supported the invasion of the Falkland Islands by the Argentine military dictator in 1982 and blessed it as a Christian undertaking.

The Church's move from being a pillar of the establishment to being a critic of the status quo was not achieved without a good deal of disruption and bitterness and the transition is still not fully completed. An instance of how bitter feelings could become was provided in 1977 by a public altercation between two well-known Brazilian bishops who found themselves on opposing sides of the barricade. Geraldo de Proença Sigaud, Archbishop of the city of Diamantina, became famous for his support of an extreme conservative group Tradition, Family and Property which was founded in Brazil and later spread to other countries in southern South America. The political ethos of TFP was precisely that of the crusades; the members saw themselves as medieval military champions of Christendom willing to do battle for what they saw as 'Western Christian civilisation' against Marxism and Socialism and in defence of private property. They eulogised García Moreno whom they wanted to be declared a saint. The movement had strong support from a number of Brazilian millionaires and all those who had an interest in opposing higher taxation. The medieval ethos was reflected even in the cloth banners which were carried in TFP's combative public meetings.

Sigaud's opponent was Pedro Casaldaliga, a Catalan born near Barcelona, who had become bishop of a rural area, São Félix de Araguaia, which contained a great many Indians. A combative man whose life was lived among the poorest of Brazilians, Casaldaliga saw the oppressiveness of the landlords during the military dictatorship and was willing to make open protests at a time when such protests were taken ipso facto as evidence of communism. He received a number of threats for his pains. Two of his own diocesan priests were murdered.

Sigaud got together a large compendium of the more outspoken statements of Casaldaliga and another bishop, Tomás Balduino of Goiás. These – which included Casaldaliga's poem in praise of Ché Guevara and criticisms of Brazil's landed estates and treatment of Indians, the Vatican bureaucracy and obligatory celibacy for priests in the Latin rite of the Church – he presented to the papal nuncio. They were evidence, he said, of the bishops' pernicious

Marxism, support of Castroism and general unfitness for office. He called for Casaldaliga's deportation from Brazil. He then broadcast his views about his brother bishops through the media which, with encouragement from the military dictatorship, made much of them.

Casaldaliga and Balduino got support from the conference of Brazilian bishops but nevertheless thought it wise to go to Rome to present their case on the spot with a personal letter to Paul VI. They were not demoted and Casaldaliga was not deported. TFP lost much of its influence when there was a return to civilian rule in Brazil.

In general there was persecution of the Church after the military putsch of 1964. Priests and lay people who opposed the putsch on religious grounds were threatened, imprisoned, tortured and killed and the bishop of one industrial town outside Rio de Janeiro was put on trial for 'subversion'.

The military continued to be hostile to the new Brazilian Church even after they handed power back to a constitutional civilian government in 1985. In a document prepared by the military in 1987 and leaked to a newspaper, the generals accused the Church leadership of being a radical minority 'which advocates social improvement for the neediest sectors of the population while preaching the use of force, mass movements and rapid and radical social changes and keeping the conservative majority of the Church cowed'. It proposed greater controls on religious organisations, foreign priests and foreign funding of Church campaigns.

The most famous victim of conservative anger against the Church has, however, been Archbishop Oscar Romero of San Salvador. Never a radical by temperament, Romero had been borne along by the changes in the Church and become increasingly critical of Salvadorean society with its tight concentration of wealth in few hands and indigence for the great majority. He had also come to fear United States military involvement in his country as Washington intervened in a growing civil war seeking to bolster up the status quo and guard against any advance by the left. On 17 February 1980, he read out in the cathedral the draft of a letter he intended to send President Carter begging him to halt military aid to the army which, he said, would 'undoubtedly sharpen the injustice and the repression of the organised people, whose struggle has often been for the respect of their most basic human rights.' The congregation in the ugly half-finished concrete cathedral applauded and he sent it off that day. On Sunday 23 March he had words for the armed forces. 'In the name of God, and in the name of this suffering people whose laments rise to heaven every day more tumultuous, I beg you, I ask you, I order you in the name of God: Stop the repression.'

The next day, one second after he had finished the homily at the mass he was saying in a private chapel at a local hospital, a single shot rang out from the doorway. With blood pouring from his nose and mouth he fell to the ground behind the altar. They got him to the emergency room at the Policlínica but there he died drowning in his own blood, the bullet still lodged in his ribs. A few days later at his funeral which was attended by dignitaries from many countries the mourning crowds were machine-gunned and forty more died on the steps of the cathedral. No one has ever been charged with the assassination of Romero or with the deaths of the forty.

Not all the opposition to liberation theology has been violent. Much has come from conservatives within the Church. The most formidable has been Cardinal Alfonso López Trujillo, Archbishop of Medellín, a Colombian prelate who was secretary and later president of CELAM, the Latin American Bishops' Conference. He made no attempt to hide his rejection of liberation theologians' views and, as he was at the centre of the spider's web, was often able to put a brake on their initiatives. His promotion to the rank of cardinal, like that of Mgr Obando, the anti-Sandinista archbishop of Managua, was seen as a sign of the Vatican's unhappiness with those of advanced views. Another opponent has been Boaventura Kloppenburg who was made auxiliary bishop of the big and poor Brazilian diocese of Salvador. The third is Roger Vekemans, a very controversial Belgian priest who was a prominent supporter of the Christian Democrats when he lived in Chile and a deadly enemy of the left-wing government of Dr Salvador Allende.

In 1984 the Vatican issued instructions which were, in part, critical of the liberation theologians. But more recently John Paul has given the impression of becoming a little more indulgent towards the movement. At the end of a marathon consultation with the 370 Brazilian bishops, which went on over a period of 14 months, the Pope came out with a message to them in April 1986 in which he said, 'We and you are convinced that the theology of liberation is not only opportune but also useful and necessary', though he went on to add somewhat menacingly, 'May God help you to be increasingly watchful that this correct and necessary theology of liberation develops in Brazil and in Latin America in a way which is homogenous and not heterogeneous with the theology of all ages.'

Some, however, are still doubtful of the Pope's attitudes. On his 1987 visit to the United States he landed first in Miami with its communities of right-wing and often violent anti-Castro and anti-Sandinista émigrés. This prompted a tart comment from Casaldaliga.

'Reagan,' he said, 'said that John Paul II could give the Americans useful advice, above all because he had experienced communism and nazism at close quarters. I'd like to add that John Paul II hasn't had close experience of Reagan's imperialism in Central America. That is why the Vatican and Pope John Paul II haven't got the receptivity I think they should have for liberation theology and the problems of our communities.'

Liberation theology is now too well established to wither at the frown of a pope. As it develops it is having effects outside the Latin American Catholic community. It is certainly gaining currency among other Third World churches, Catholic and Protestant. In 1976 the Ecumenical Association of Third World Theologians was set up and has held conferences in a number of cities from Dar es Salaam and Accra to São Paulo and Geneva. At all of them, the influence of the Latin Americans has been very great.

Within the region, discussion of the frontiers of the orthodoxy have lead Catholic theologians to greater co-operation with their Protestant counterparts. Protestants such as José Miguez Bonino and Emilio Castro have gained reputations as creative thinkers which are on a par with the Catholics and this has brought together religious traditions which would often have been mutually hostile.

## Non-Catholic religions

Liberation theology, however, has not had any effect on the many fundamentalist Protestant groups and sects, such as the Mormons, who are bitterly opposed to all the Catholic Church, radical or conservative, stands for. Many missionaries of these groups have entered from the United States, often with the encouragement of right-wing political extremists there. In 1982 a group of advisers to President Reagan submitted a series of policy recommendations to him which they called, with conscious or unconscious irony, the Santa Fé (Holy Faith) Document. One of the recommendations suggested, 'American foreign policy must begin to counter-attack (and not just react against) liberation theology.' The Document was taken seriously in Washington and as a result there was founded an Institute for Religion and Democracy whose prime job was to confront the liberation theologians. The Institute has been working in parallel with the United States fundamentalist sects. These sects have taken strong root in the military regimes of Central America and had a particular heyday in the early 1980s during the dictatorship of General Efraín Ríos Montt, the Guatemalan who declared himself to be a 'born-again Christian'. Despite the great media coverage they organise, their effect is often little more than spasmodic.

Neither has liberation theology had much effect so far on the popular 'spiritist' religions of Brazil, Cuba and Haïti where the beliefs the blacks brought with them from Africa are still strong. Voodoo is widespread in Haïti. Its various roots are still traceable to the religions of Dahomey, Nigeria, Togo and the Congo and the traditions of the Fon and Yoruba peoples in particular. There is some mixing of Christian beliefs with the old African ones.

In colonial times the French Church clearly had little time or energy to devote to preaching to the slaves, and the slaves had little time for it when they rose in revolt against their white masters. Boukman, one of the founders of the independent Haïtian nation in the late eighteenth century, was a voodoo priest or *houngan* and many of Haïti's rulers, not least the Duvaliers, have been active in voodoo. Rome, for its part, suffers still for its political decision to boycott and not to recognise or come to terms with the country's black government for decades from its independence till late in the nineteenth century.

In Brazil the African religions have not only held their own, they have affected the religious beliefs of those with little or no African blood in their veins, of middle-class people as well as poorer people. The original African spiritism is known as Macumba or Umbanda, while a more intellectual set of spiritist beliefs are based on the writings of a nineteenth-century Frenchman from Lyon, Hippolyte-Léon-Denizard Rivail, who wrote under the name of Allan Kardec.

An academic study of the beliefs of the slum-dwellers of Rio de

Janeiro in 1958 showed that 83 per cent declared they were Catholics and more than 98 per cent had their children baptised in Catholic churches. Nevertheless two-thirds of the slum-dwellers said they went to Umbanda sessions, three-quarters believed in charms and spells and 62 per cent had faith in witchcraft.

The Church itself realises that the prevalence of spiritism stems in great part from the defects in Catholicism from colonial times onwards. When the African came to Brazil, Kloppenburg has argued, he found 'a Catholicism very strongly fettered to superstitious customs and practices, a Catholicism which really confused charms and talismans with medals, reliquaries and sacramentals . . . And this type of Catholicism which still predominates today is not, in fact, an authentic Christianity but is more akin to African fetishism itself. And since 33 per cent of our Brazilian population has African blood, all of this great portion of our population was almost naturally drawn to Umbanda, which represented itself as "the religion of Brazil".'

Umbanda is everywhere to be seen in a city like Rio de Janeiro. On the magnificent Atlantic beaches of Copacabana and Ipanema, filled during the day with the bronzed bodies of athletes and sunlovers, candles will be lit and left to appease the gods at dusk. In the jungle park of Tijuca a few minutes' drive from the centre of the city, people come all day to leave offerings of cakes and drinks to the spirits at crossroads or beside waterfalls. On busy street corners there are little shrines with similar offerings. In the centres of Brazilian cities there are dozens of shops which stock the statuary and other items needed for the spiritist cults.

Kardecism is the spiritism of the drawing-room and is based on a belief in continual reincarnation. More than a century after his death, Kardec's writings are immensely popular in Brazil and translations have gone into scores of editions. His ideas have been adopted by millions of middle-class Brazilians, entrepreneurs and architects, officers and journalists.

Despite the fact that the majority of Brazilians claim to be catholics, this does not stop them from seeking direct contact with and aid from the spirit world. The Catholic church has never been reconciled to spritism in Brazil but has been virtually powerless to counter it, such a hold has it got on the majority of the population.

Brasília has been promoting itself as a world centre of the occult, 'The Capital of the Third Millenium', as it now terms itself. Some of the promoters clearly believe the publicity material. Those who do not can count the benefits to their city of attracting more visitors.

Spiritism and voodoo are not likely to have any impact outside the frontiers of the countries in which they are practised. Liberation theology, on the other hand, is likely to develop and grow increasingly influential within Latin America and outside. There is every sign that the religion which the Spanish and Portuguese took to America is coming back to challenge the guardians of orthodoxy in Rome.

# CHAPTER FIVE

# INDIANS AND BLACKS

*One of the principal reasons why conversions have become so hated by the infidels, now more than ever, is that they know that to accept our holy faith is to bow their heads and shoulders beneath the intolerable yoke of vassalage to those who are Your Majesty's own unworthy vassals.*

FRAY FRANCISCO ROMERO, EIGHTEENTH-CENTURY MISSIONARY IN COLOMBIA

*The liberation of native peoples can only be brought about by the peoples themselves, or it is not liberation.*

THE DECLARATION OF BARBADOS, 1971

———

The platform of the railway station of Divisadero, high up in the Sierra Madre in the Mexican state of Chihuahua, is a cold, wet and smelly spot in the midst of tremendous natural grandeur. The mist rises up out of the Copper Canyon, a great cleft in the land, deeper and more wooded than the Grand Canyon to the north in the United States. For many centuries the pine-covered land around has been the home of the Tarahumara Indians, famous for their powers of long-distance running. The Aztecs, who never conquered them, appreciated them as messengers who were able, it is said, to run for three days at a time non-stop.

The daily trains, one down to the city of Chihuahua, the other down to the Pacific Ocean, have been and gone. A few Tarahumaras have gathered on the platform for the benefit of a small group of

117

tourists, Mexicans and foreigners staying at the nearby hotel which overlooks the Canyon. The women have brought handicrafts to sell, little boxes perfectly woven out of plant fibre. The babies have been put down by their mothers in cardboard boxes to cough and sniffle in the drizzle.

A few listless Tarahumara men eventually turn up and, after much haggling over money with Pepe, the tour guide, go into a shuffling routine to the accompaniment of a scraping violin.

'Qué maravilla!' says the elderly lady from Chihuahua.

The proceedings finish with a demonstration of giggling Tarahumara girls racing in teams, throwing coloured wooden hoops in front of them.

Pepe does his best to inject the excitement of a greyhound track into the dismal scene. 'Come on, the Reds,' he cries. 'Somebody shout for the Blues.'

By now the Tarahumara men have shuffled back to their shacks on the hill overlooking the station to wait for the next day's dispiriting and embarrassing performance. The babies are carted away and the tourists go back with their native knicknacks to the hotel's great log fire and their whiskies.

## Ancient civilisations

Five hundred years ago the native peoples of Latin America began to be conquered by the Europeans. Today these people, whom Columbus called 'Indians' because he thought he had reached the East Indies, are beginning to unite and fight back for their rights. The form of their struggle takes different forms, some cultural, some political, some military, and depends on the widely differing circumstances of the different peoples. The outcome is still far from being settled. But there can be no doubt that the fight has started – or, better – has been renewed.

The first tribes to populate the region came from Asia across the Bering Strait to what is now Alaska about 35000 BC and there is evidence that, 15000 years later, they had penetrated as far as Mexico. At birth many of the native peoples bear the Mongol spot, a blue spot at the base of the spine which disappears after a few months, and this characteristic is evidence of their distant relationship to the Mongoloid peoples of Asia who also bear it. From Alaska the earliest settlers fanned out southwards till they reached the remote and cold southern extremities of the continent.

*The Maya*   By the time Columbus arrived in 1492 to conquer and convert the original peoples to Christianity, many empires had come and gone in the region. The most remarkable of these were the older civilisations of Mexico and Central America (Meso-America as the archaeologists term it) and in particular the Maya civilisation. The Maya have been called the Greeks of America. The ruins of their buildings – pyramids, temples and palaces – and the sculpture and pottery with which they adorned them bear witness to the beauty and delicacy of their culture. Little sign has been found of dwellings within their cities. The deduction must be therefore that they had the resources and leisure to erect great cere-monial centres around which they themselves lived. They were fascinated by the calculation of the passage of time and their mathematical skills were amazing: they computed in hundreds of millions of years and had developed the concept of zero well before it was discovered in India. They commemorated the deeds of their kings in hieroglyphics which scholars are only just succeeding in deciphering. Though they were astronomers and architects, they did not use the arch or the wheel and used metal rarely.

By the time the Spaniards arrived, the Maya had long been in decline. Their settlements were overgrown and their cities deserted as the result of some chronic disaster, natural or man-made, which took place around AD 1000 and which we do not yet fully comprehend. It was not till the middle of the last century that explorers began rediscovering the remains of their civilisation and, with the jungles continually yielding up new evidence, we are still a long way from getting a full picture of their culture. The folk memories which their descendants retain of this period of greatness are hazy at best and throw little light on the civilisation. But there is no doubt that the Maya were responsible for artistic achievement of a very high order indeed.

*The Aztecs*   Another two civilisations were in full flower at the time the Spaniards came. The Aztecs had founded an empire whose centre was the city of Tenochtitlán, which so impressed Bernal Díaz del Castillo, and which stretched a thousand kilometres from north to south. The Aztec civilisation was an altogether more sombre one than that of the Maya. The Aztecs' history had, accord-ing to their own account, been one of suffering and enslavement to other peoples which had been alleviated by the help and guidance they received from their gods. John Edwin Fagg, the US historian, described their religion thus:

> The Aztec religion was truly a horrifying affair by the standards of any time. In centers all over Mexico, prisoners waited in cages until the grim Aztec officials arrived to send them on to Tenochtitlán. In that spectacular city, at least every twenty days groups were dragged or forced up the pyramid steps while yelling, drunken Aztecs danced grue-somely about the base. The usual method of sacrifice was for the priests to throw the victim on his back upon a large stone, break open his chest with a dull obsidian blade, and tear out his heart. The heart might then be eaten by the clergy, the victim's skin taken and used for dress in jest, mockery or even reverence, and his skull placed in a hideous collection that grew to monstrous proportions. Macabre variations to this procedure featured ceremonies at the beginning of each eighteen months. Sometimes the victim would have to fight with feathers against armed warriors until they killed him by degrees. One particularly cruel celebration involved roasting the prisoners before they were finally killed. Some of the victims were children, a few were women, a still smaller number were honored prisoners, but by far the most were anonymous prisoners of war. They died by the thousand. In the reign of Montezuma II, twenty thousand were said to have been killed in a single ceremony. These mass executions were occasion for great rejoicing by the Aztec people.

For sixty years before Cortés arrived, the Aztecs had been at the height of their power. The subject peoples from whom they exacted tribute, needless to say, hated them and did not need much encouragement to side with the Spaniards in helping to overthrow them. They were no match for the horses, firearms and armour of the invaders.

*The Incas*  An even greater and older civilisation awaited the Spaniards in the Andes. The Incas, like the Aztecs, were at the height of their powers, the latest in a long line of civilisations which had flourished in the mountains and along the coasts of what is now Peru. Their emperor, the Sapa Inca, was the son of the sun and worshipped by his subjects. From their capital in Cuzco, 'the navel of the world', they ruled an area which dwarfed the Aztec domains and which today contains most of the territory of Peru, Ecuador, Bolivia and Chile and a large part of Argentina. The Incas, however, were less harsh, more efficient rulers than the Aztecs and governed through local chiefs where they could. From the navel of the world runners came and went with the imperial dispatches along paved roads, across the rope bridges which spanned the wild Andean rivers or with the aid of markers along the routes over the deserts. They also had a highly developed work ethic, organising their subjects into efficient labour forces and growing and distributing food for all. They did not use the wheel and had no writing, recording facts on the *quipu*, a series of pieces of string with mulicoloured knots which were made and interpreted by experts.

Their monuments have none of the grace and beauty of the Maya ruins and artefacts. They do have a massive solidity. In Cuzco, Sacsahuamán and Machu Picchu they put together blocks of stone weighing hundreds of tons, cut with such skill that to this day it is not possible to put a knife blade between them. For centuries these massive walls have defied the earthquakes which have brought down the flimsier constructions of the Europeans. How the Incas moved these stones up mountains and across rivers with no draught animals and no pulleys, with the unaided strength of human muscle, is a source of wonderment to anyone who sees them.

## The arrival of the Europeans

The Spaniard who in 1532 brought the Incas low, a former swineherd called Francisco Pizarro, was a ruffian and an adventurer. He had the good luck to get to Peru at a time when Atahualpa and Huáscar, the two sons of the late emperor, were fighting for the throne. His soldiers attacked the Inca court at Cajamarca to the predictable war cry of 'Santiago!' Pizarro captured Atahualpa and held him to ransom for a room filled with gold and another filled with silver. When the ransom was in, Pizarro had him killed, he and his men thus becoming rich as well as powerful. The first of many Inca rebellions flared under the last emperor, Manco Cápac, whom Pizarro thought would be his puppet. But the revolt petered out and the greatest empire the western hemisphere had seen was gone.

The incoming Europeans encountered many other native Americans. None had the grandeur of the Aztecs or the Incas, some wore skins, others went naked, but they populated, albeit often very lightly, every part of the region from the Amazon jungles to Tierra del Fuego. The vast majority of them were destined to perish by European swords, European diseases – influenza and smallpox – or out of the sheer melancholy and despair which overtakes a community when it sees its culture and its way of life shattered for ever by a foreign power.

*The Tainos*  The Tainos, the inhabitants of Hispaniola, the first big island colonised by the Spaniards, were the first victims. Their fate was typical of that of any small indigenous communities. They were simple people who produced simple but pleasing pottery and wore ornaments of the native gold and not much else. The gold caught the eye of the first colonists, who put the Tainos to forced labour digging it. Such was the shock to the people that they started to commit mass suicide by drinking the poisonous juice of the yellow yucca, hanging themselves, killing their own children so that they would not grow up in such calamitous circumstances and urging their wives to end their pregnancies. Of the 600000 who were alive in 1492 when Columbus arrived, no more than 60000 survived until 1508 when a census was taken. By 1517 they were down to 11000, ruled by about 700 Spaniards. A two-month epidemic of smallpox, which started in December 1518, pushed the number down to 3000. By that time the gold that was accessible was almost exhausted. The Tainos were completely wiped out by 1550. Montesinos had preached in vain.

*Slaves from Africa*  Workers had to be got from somewhere, especially when it was discovered that sugar could be grown easily and fetch high prices in Europe. In 1518 there started a trade in black slaves from Africa which was to transform Hispaniola and much of the rest of the Caribbean basin and Brazil. The trade was to grow and grow. In the first part of the seventeenth century slavers brought over an average of 3000 slaves a year to Spain's American dominions. By the end of the century the average had risen to 6600 a year. Eight thousand slaves a year arrived in Brazil throughout most of the seventeenth century. At the end of the eighteenth century there were years in which the French were importing no less than 40000 slaves to work on the extraordinarily profitable plantations of Saint-Domingue (now known as Haïti), the western third of the island of Hispaniola which they had taken from the Spaniards in 1697. In the sugar growing areas of the north-east of Brazil two-thirds of the population was black. In the 1780s there were about 30000 whites in Saint-Domingue to 27500 free slaves and mulattos and 465000 slaves. All over the region the slaves were condemned to a sub-human life. They arrived in ships which were floating coffins and lived under a fatal regime of labour and degradation. There were many more men of marriageable age than women, the slave owners did not encourage matrimony and were not keen on the expense of feeding black babies who could not work.

As the blacks arrived from Africa so the Indian population withered. Some, like the Tainos, disappeared completely. Others all but vanished. When Cortés reached the heartland of Mexico in 1519, the population was, according to scholars' estimates, 25000000. Sixty years later it was down to less than 2000000. In 1530 the northern Andes had a population of 10000000. Sixty years later it had dropped to 1500000. Abortions rose and the birth rate fell in many places. The enormity of the cataclysm which overtook the native peoples can be imagined only with difficulty, a series of genocides which in numbers far outstrip the killing of the Jews by the Nazis under Hitler.

The aggression by the Europeans continued to the nineteenth century and, in isolated places, is still going on today. In southern Chile, the Araucanians or Mapuches held out for centuries against the Europeans as they had earlier held out against the Incas. They kept both sets of invaders north of the Bío-Bío River. But by the 1880s they had been reduced by the combined effects of modern weapons, a flood of European immigrants, the building of a trunk railway through their lands and a tide of alcohol. Of an estimated 1000000 indigenes at the time of the Spanish conquest of Chile, there were no more than 50000 by 1890.

At about the same time the Argentine government sent a military expedition to Patagonia which massacred all but a few indigenes, the survivors being shunted off to reservations. In our own day the pressure of European settlers invading the interior of Brazil, Paraguay, Peru and Ecuador has disrupted the lives of jungle Indians who have previously had the forests and wildernesses to themselves. In the Brazilian Amazon the indigenous races have withdrawn further and further into the bush away from the encroaching Europeans and the blacks.

## Native resistance

But the European onslaught on the freedoms and beliefs of the indigenes was at many times and in many places the object of resistance. In some communities, such as the Tainos, that resistance was despairing and unavailing. In others it was tenacious and bloody.

*Tupac Amaru II* The greatest challenge ever to Spain's rule in America came in 1780 when a descendant of the Inca imperial family declared himself to be the rightful leader of the Inca peoples under the name Tupac Amaru II. Right down the Andes, including those areas such as modern Venezuela and southern Chile which were never part of the Inca empire, natives rose up against their colonial masters, killing and butchering in a riot of atrocity and revenge. Interestingly the rebels did not say that one of their aims was the overthrow of Christianity, they said merely that they wanted to see the Christian principles that the white men preached put into practice. Tupac Amaru himself was betrayed, captured by the Spaniards and executed by being pulled apart by horses in 1781, but the revolt went on for years. The city of La Paz, filled with shivering Europeans and mestizos, was besieged twice but the rising was eventually put down because the Spaniards continued to have full military superiority over their subject peoples.

*Haïti* It was, however, the blacks, the descendants of the first slaves brought to Hispaniola, who staged the first successful revolt. By the end of the eighteenth century the French colony of Saint-Domingue had become stupendously rich and profitable from the sugar trade. In the 1790s the blacks rose up, murdered the whites who had been killing them and by 1801 had set up their own republic – the second free republic in America after the United States and the first black republic of modern times. The shock waves that lapped around the Caribbean from this event were enormous. That shock increased when the Haïtians took over the Spanish-speaking two-thirds of the island and governed it for two decades. France refused to recognise the loss of its colony till 1825 and then sent fourteen men-of-war to demand compensation of 150000000 francs, a sum which paupered the country.

Haïti has struggled on. The sight of an independent black state in the Caribbean was poison to the slave-owning states of the United States which were worried at the example the country gave of black power. After continual interference by the US Navy, Haïti was formally occupied by the United States from 1915 to 1934. Not long after that it fell into the hands of the Duvalier dynasty. Even at the best of times the Haïtians have few friends in the region: the lessons to be drawn from the republic's history are still too painful for whites.

*The Maya*　The struggle of the Maya, too, is going on to this day. There were revolts against Spanish rule among Maya in what is now Guatemala in the eighteenth century; and the Maya of Yucatán, the easternmost part of Mexico which sticks into the Caribbean, rose in revolt in 1847. Drawing on their own folklore which had been collected in a book, the *Chilam Balam*, compiled just after the coming of the Spaniards, the Maya looked for leadership to their 'talking cross'. The talking cross was at a shrine where the elders of the race would give out their message to the fighters as though it came from God. The messages to the faithful and the rebel soldiers often assured them that they would be invulnerable to the bullets of the Mexican army. The rebellion was not finally put down till 1901.

*Colombia*　The struggle of the Indians has often thrown up leaders who would have distinguished themselves in any circumstances. One such was Manuel Quintín Lame, who carried on a fight which was at times military, at times political, but at all times relentless in the defence and recovery of the lands and the protection of the customs of the Indians of Colombia. He never had any formal schooling but had a mystical belief in his own powers and in the justice and the final triumph of the Indian cause once the indigenes had been awakened to it. He was convinced of the superior intelligence of the Indian. His campaign started in 1910 in the wide valley of the Cauca River and did not end till his death. On 9 May 1915 he was betrayed and captured by the Colombian authorities, who kept him in leg irons for a year in the jail at Popayán. Under his influence a Supreme Council of Indians was set up in Colombia in 1920.

He was forced from his native valley but then went to live in the neighbouring department of Tolima where the Indians were in even worse conditions than in the Cauca valley. With a group of Indian companions he set up an Indian reservation with its own school and adult education. In 1931 the government and the land-owners stormed it at the cost of 17 dead and 37 wounded, and Lame was put in prison for another two years.

Lame went on fighting for the Indians' cause, dictating his thoughts to an amanuensis until he died in 1967. He had some practical pieces of advice for the Indians. These included:

'Do not believe in the friendship of the white man or the mestizo.

Distrust gifts and flattery.

Never consult a white lawyer.

Do not allow yourself to be hoodwinked by the chattering politicians of any party.'

*Guatemala*   In Guatemala, where the majority of the population are Indian by blood, the fighting is continuing still. Four million of the country's 7000000 people have a mother tongue which is not Spanish. They are divided into 23 language groups. The majority of the rest of the population are Ladinos, people with some European blood in their veins. In 1954 the elected president of the country, Jacobo Arbenz, was overthrown by a right-wing military group backed by the United States after US bombers had raided Guatemala City. Not a communist himself but one who was pre-pared to co-operate with communists in bringing some reforms to Guatemala, Arbenz made the mistake of ordering arms from Eastern Europe. That decision provided the occasion to overthrow him. It took eight years for a guerrilla riposte to be mounted to Arbenz's overthrow but since then fighting, though badly reported in the foreign press, has been continuous.

Three guerrilla bands, loosely allied in a confederation known as the URNG (Guatemalan National Revolutionary Union), are in action against an army over which the elected government of President Vinicio Cerezo has little or no control. At least eight out of ten of the members of these bands are Indians, the majority from races con-nected to the Maya racial group. This forgotten war began as a political struggle and has developed into a racial war with ideological overtones.

In May 1978 the Guatemalan army staged a massacre of Indians which became a byword for violence even in a society familiar with violence. Kekchi Indians aiming to protest against the take-over of their ancestral lands converged on the town of Panzós to lobby the municipal authorities. More than a hundred were mown down by machine-gun fire from the army, their corpses shoved onto municipal refuse lorries and dumped in mass graves. The machine-gun emplacements had been set up and the mass graves scooped out by bulldozers before the demonstration took place.

The ferocity of the war can be measured by the fact that, in the six years from 1980, 60000 lost their lives and 440 villages were destroyed. The war has caused 500000 Guatemalans to flee their homes, with 150000 crossing the border into Mexico and the rest becoming refugees in their own country. One particular community, the Ixil, who numbered 45000 in 1969 and who were prominent in the resistance to the military regimes, has virtually disappeared. In November 1982 Americas Watch, a United States human rights organisation, reported, 'One of the 23 linguistic groups, the Ixil in El Quiché has been all but wiped out as a cultural entity.' The URNG is the heir of those Maya who from the earliest days of Spanish conquest resisted foreign rule.

*Brazil* The Indians have found other, less violent, ways of resisting. Native populations have been growing gradually in many places. On its foundation in 1971, the Survival International organisation in London was forecasting that by 1981 all the Indians in the Brazilian Amazon would have died out. In 1987 the organisation was able to report that there were still 220000 Indians living in the country. More indigenous peoples had been hidden away out of contact with the white man than had been thought and foreign public opinion, alerted by lobbying groups such as Survival International itself, had prevailed on the Brazilian government to change its policy of absorption of the indigenes and the exploitation of their lands. Many of the Indians of Brazil, especially those living near the frontiers, are in danger from 'the military's preoccupation with what they call 'national security' and the army's perceived need to populate the border zones with less primitive peoples. But they have survived at least this far.

*Chile*   The Araucanians reached their lowest point in 1890 with 50000 but, recovering perhaps from the shock of having white men on their land for the first time, have been increasing in numbers since then. The exact figures have been the subject of controversy. In 1964 the Chilean government Indigenous Affairs Department put the population at 400000, but in the same year another government department estimated it at no more than 173000. The Chilean foreign ministry suggested a figure of 322916. All sources however agreed that the population had been increasing.

*Paraguay*   The recovery of Paraguay, the only country of the region where a native language is in regular and common use by whites, from the depopulation of the War of the Triple Alliance is aiding the cause of Indian consciousness. Though much of the Guaraní culture has been lost, the Guaraní language still survives strongly to the point where it is the preferred language outside the capital Asunción, the newspapers print articles in Guaraní and there is even a theatre in Guaraní. From the disastrous levels of 1870, the population has recovered to nearly 4000000 and is growing at the high rate of 3.1 per cent a year. There are, too, hundreds of thousands of Paraguayans living as migrant workers in Brazil, Uruguay and Argentina.

Despite the horrors the total population even of Guatemala, Indian and non-Indian, has doubled to more than 8000000 over the past twenty years. The jungle Indians of Brazil who, according to what some ethnologists were writing only a decade ago, were expected to have been completely wiped out by now, have survived and today number about 200000 people. The total Indian population of Latin America is estimated to be about 26000000 people split up in 400 different racial groups.

## Resistance strategies

While populations have grown and guerrilla tactics have been adopted in some places a debate has gone on in and around the Indian communities about the best strategy for resistance. The Marxist view is that the indigenes' ills are the ills of capitalism and that they are only one sector of the proletariat of all races. Therefore they should, the Marxists argue, unite in a common cause with that proletariat and abandon the primitive traditions of their 'precapitalist mode of production'. To hang on to their ethnic identity is seen as swimming against the tide of history. As early as 1928 the founder of Peruvian communism, José Carlos Mariátegui, wrote, 'Why should the Inca people, which invented the most elaborate and harmonious system of communism, alone be insensible to the movement which is stirring up the Chinese and Indians of Asia?'

*The Barbados Declaration* Another powerful school of thought argues that liberation demands the assertion and preservation of ethnic values. That approach received support at the meeting of anthropologists held in Barbados in 1971 under the aegis of the World Council of Churches and whose final Declaration became a key political document in the debate on the indigenes' future. Though it sprang from a Church body, the Barbados Declaration did not hesitate to castigate the missionaries for their view of the Indians as 'pagan and heretical', for their demand for 'submission in exchange for future supernatural compensations' and for their collaboration with 'dominant imperial interests'.

'As a result of this analysis,' the Declaration went on to say, 'we conclude that the suspension of all missionary activity is the most appropriate policy for the good of Indian society and for the moral integrity of the Churches involved.' Though the Declaration did not have a fraction of the weight it would have commanded had it been produced under the aegis of the Catholic Church, it could not fail to have a good deal of impact.

*The Aguaruna and Huambisa Council* Since the Barbados Declaration there has been a strong growth of political activity by indigenous groups working within the framework of existing European-dominated societies to achieve recognition for their needs and improve the circumstances of their daily life. The Aguaruna and the Huambisa, for instance, are two groups totalling 35 000 people who live from hunting, fishing and slash-and-burn agriculture in the forests in an area the size of Wales on the Ecuador–Peru border. They formed a joint council of their 100 communities in 1977 to fight for land rights, better health and better education. So expert in lobbying have they become that they regularly seek advice and aid from British organisations such as Christian Aid and the Catholic Institute for International Relations who have sent volunteer doctors to live among them and help them. The Aguaruna and

Huambisa are now hoping to send their own people to train as doctors.

The Aguaruna and Huambisa Council is one of a dozen similar organisations which represent about half the 220000 jungle Indians in Peru. These organisations have themselves come together under an umbrella AIDESEP, the Inter-Ethnic Association of the Peruvian Jungle. AIDESEP is governed by an assembly of representatives which meets every six months; and its president, an Aguaruna called Evaristo Nugkuag, was recently awarded the alternative Nobel Peace Prize. The award exemplifed the support that the indigenes' cause has awakened in the world at large.

Several times representatives of indigenous communities from various countries, including the United States and Canada, have come together in international conferences to pool their knowledge and expertise.

*The Senderistas*　One fearsome guerrilla movement, the Sendero Luminoso in Peru, has purposefully sought to marry Indian consciousness with combative Marxism–Leninism. Sendero was founded at Ayacucho in 1970 by Abimael Guzmán, or 'Comrade Gonzalo', a professor at the local university. Guzmán, an admirer of Mao Tse-Tung and not himself an Indian, has built up a core of fanatically devoted followers, the majority of whom are Indians. They regard him as 'the fourth sword of Marxism', in succession to Marx himself, Lenin and Mao, and hold in contempt revisionists such as Fidel Castro, Kim Il Sung of North Korea and the late Enver Hoxha of Albania. Guzmán himself, who was born in 1934, has been in hiding for many years and it is not certain whether he is alive or dead. In the service of what they consider the purest communist doctrine left in the world the Senderistas have, since 1980, pursued a very violent struggle against the Peruvian state and in particular against those with European blood who are regarded as 'foreigners'. They regard their struggle as being in direct descent from that of Tupac Amaru II – though they clearly reject his view of Christianity. In the first eight years of their struggle they were estimated to have killed 8000 people. The government response has been equally violent. In June 1986 there were mutinies by Sendero prisoners at two men's and a women's prison. President Alan García sent in the army and, according to official figures, 249 of the prisoners were killed, some after they had surrendered. In

December 1987 to 'celebrate' the anniversary of the foundation of their organisation, the Senderistas killed two mayors, a Civil Guard and a priest while he said mass and placed bombs on electricity pylons and cut off communications with six provinces in the Andes by blowing bridges and cutting telephone lines.

Though there is not yet peace between the races in Latin America the worst, it seems, is over for the indigenous peoples. It may be that a few of the tiniest Indian communities, those who are reduced to a score of men and women, will tragically but peacefully die out. It could be that there will be some more cases of deliberate genocide of comparatively small groups, such as the Ixil in Guatemala. But it is inconceivable that there could be a killing such as occurred in the first years of the sixteenth century of the Tainos on Hispaniola. The native peoples are by now beginning to be conscious of their rights and are, in different ways, starting to claim them. The challenge which faces them is that of choosing those products of the more technically advanced Western culture which can benefit them – medicines and well-planned education, for instance – and rejecting others – from alcohol to fundamentalist Christian religion – which can only destroy their cultures.

## CHAPTER SIX

# DO THEY MATTER?

*'. . . a dagger pointing at the heart of Antarctica'.*
HENRY KISSINGER

'If Latin America were to sink beneath the ocean this afternoon, not many people in Europe would notice,' one pessimistic Latin American economist said to me in December 1987. By many reckonings he would be right. Though familiarity with Latin America has grown markedly in Britain and the rest of Europe over the past two or three decades, the Europeans' knowledge of the politics of Latin America remains patchy. Europeans have a fair idea who are the aggressors and who are the victims in Central America, just as they had a clear idea of which side they supported at the time of General Pinochet's putsch against the elected government of Chile in 1973. But knowledge of other areas is fuzzier.

Nor is there any clear realisation outside Latin America of the scale of Latin American achievement in many spheres. Despite the disastrous period of military rule through which Argentina and Uruguay have passed, the general level of culture and literacy in these two countries is probably higher than it is in Britain. Beside the incompetent and lazy companies which do exist in the region, Pemex, Petrobras and Petróleos de Venezuela, for instance, are among the biggest oil companies in the world. They are trading competently in their home markets and abroad without the supervision of foreign multinationals. If at the end of the Second World War anyone had predicted that within forty years Latin Americans would be selling aircraft to the British Post Office and the Royal Air Force he would hardly have been believed. Yet Embraer of Brazil has done just that.

Despite occasional commercial coups, however, trade generally is not flourishing. British exporters, for instance, sell more to Denmark every year than they sell to the whole of Latin America – and British trade with the region is declining. Indeed, Latin America's trading importance to Europe as a whole is shrinking, as the EEC's Common Agricultural Policy makes it self-sufficient in, and an exporter of, products such as cereals and meat which fifty years ago were imported from Latin America in large quantities.

While the Latin Americans have been cutting their consumption and reducing their imports drastically in an effort to meet the payment terms to the banks on their big foreign debts, European governments and trade unions have been slow to protest. They have failed to make the point that a reduction in Latin America's ability to import goods has meant a loss of many jobs in European factories. They do not point out that had the Latin Americans continued to import at the rate they did before the debt crisis in 1982, there might have been one million fewer unemployed in Europe.

Nor are European investments in Latin America as important to either side as they were in the nineteenth century when European money poured into the region to create railways and roads, factories and farms, and in the process paid handsome dividends. The way Latin Americans treat the £82 000 000 000 in foreign loans made to them by British and other European banks is certainly important for the banks' health. But even here the banks are beginning to reconcile themselves to the fact that they will not be repaid on time and that there is little they can do about it. They are rapidly making provision for their bad debts.

Nor, since the very acute Cuban missile crisis of 1962, has Latin America been a major source of international tension comparable to, say, the Middle East, Korea, Berlin or Vietnam. Even the Reagan administration's professed anxiety over Nicaragua as a possible base for Soviet attack on the United States rings hollow. The Central American crisis, which has taken up so much of the attention of the Reagan administration, is clearly more the result of the poverty and repression imposed on the people of Central

America by dictatorial government, very often backed by the United States itself, than of the machinations of Moscow. For its part the Soviet Union, which in 1987 cut its shipments of oil to Nicaragua at a time when the Sandinista government was facing increasing threats from foreign-financed terrorists, has shown little inclination to commit itself deeply in Central America. Kissinger's dismissive reference to the lack of strategic importance of the region is certainly convincing to the many who see the politics of the world exclusively as a product of the interests of the United States, the USSR, Western Europe and Japan.

But the region's relative lack of importance is unlikely to continue and there is every sign that by the end of the century Latin America will be looming a great deal larger in the world than it does today. The population will be bigger and, one must presume, richer. By then, the Latin Americans should have done something to tame their military and their *caudillos* and improve the ramshackle nature of their systems of government. With cheaper and better communications they should not only have had the opportunity to forge some better regional unity. They should, too, have put the land, the sea and the subsoil to better use.

In 1960 there were 118 000 000 Latin Americans of working age; by the end of the century there will be nearly 200 000 000. Cities such as Mexico and São Paulo will have grown into even vaster conurbations than they are at the moment, each having a population of more than 30 000 000.

If the political forces which favour change and reform grow in strength, there should be progress in better distributing income. If this happens, a growing Latin American population will become a very large market for goods of all kinds, locally produced and imported.

The Latin Americans will surely have started on a more intensive exploitation of the natural resources of their region. According to some estimates, only a quarter of the usable land is being exploited today. Some of it is very difficult to make productive, much is acidic and toxic, and arable land of any sort is hard to find in the Andes, for instance. A large part of the land which is uncultivated is far from markets in cities and export ports. But even if no new land is brought into cultivation there are very big possibilities of improving the yields of that land which is at present in use. As the Inter-American Development Bank pointed out in its 1983 report,

Japan all but tripled the yield per hectare of its arable land in the eighty years to 1960. Farmers in Latin America are realising that they, too, can improve their yields; and the amount of fertilisers they are using is growing rapidly every year.

Latin America has, too, great quantities of water. (The wettest place in the world is the department of Chocó in Colombia near the Panamanian border, where eight metres of rain fall every year.) A third of the water that drains into the world's oceans comes from Latin America, notably from the Amazon which, at its mouth, is more a sea than a river. Very large quantities of electricity could be generated from all that water, but only about 7 per cent of the hydroelectric potential is put to use.

With a third of the area of Latin America under forest, the region is beginning to be a major world supplier of paper, timber and other wood products. In fishing the South Atlantic, to take one example, is a goldmine for trawlers which come to the waters around the Falklands from all over the world, to catch everything from whiting to squid.

And Latin America still has enormous quantities of minerals, the substances which brought the Spaniards in the first place – a quarter of the world's copper and bauxite, a fifth of the world's silver and iron ore, and even bigger shares of exotic metals such as molybdenum, antimony and lithium. As far as fuels are concerned the region is a big net exporter of petroleum and natural gas; and the world's biggest coalmine, on the Caribbean coast of Colombia, will soon be competing hard for business with the collieries of Europe.

The economies of Latin America and Europe consequently complement each other. On the one hand are the Europeans, continually worried about the sources of raw materials for their factories and about finding markets for the goods they produce. On the other are Latin Americans eager to industrialise further. They pay for the sophisticated machinery they need by selling the raw materials they do not themselves consume and whatever manufactured products they can turn out.

The future of Latin America will sooner or later concern Europeans for broader reasons than just those of trade. No other part of the Third World is as close to Europe as Latin America is. The ties of language, culture and religion between Latin America and Europe are still strong and indeed gaining in strength.

However much their good intentions are broken, the majority of Latin Americans subscribe – or would subscribe, if given the opportunity – to the values of human rights as preached in Europe today and as set out long ago by the Montesinos' and the Vieiras.

The echoes of European politics too are, as we have seen, everywhere to be heard within Latin America. The adoption of Western European political models, as Latin America's politics have begun to evolve away from *caudillos* and strong men, is one sign of a receptivity to European ideas. Democratic socialism of the kind associated with the British Labour Party and the socialist parties of West Germany, Scandinavia, Italy, Spain and Portugal, Christian democracy such as is found in Italy and West Germany, and a certain rather old-fashioned liberalism, have all been widely adopted in the region. In Venezuela, once a byword for dictatorship, Christian democracy and democratic socialism have been alternating in power. A Christian democratic government won a landslide victory in Chile in 1964 and – somewhat unwillingly, to be sure – passed over power to the democratically elected socialist government of Salvador Allende in 1970.

Strong links between the European and Latin American followers of those political creeds have been forged within their three Internationals. Large quantities of funds have in the past flowed from European political parties to finance the election expenses or the political training of their Latin American counterparts and continue to do so.

Indeed the fact that there is now a strong flow of new ideas from Latin America which are having an impact in Europe – in the form, for instance, of the Latin American novel or of liberation theology – makes the ties even stronger than in the past. No one who aspires to keep up with the development of the modern novel can ignore the writings of Mario Vargas Llosa, Gabriel García Márquez, Carlos Fuentes or Jorge Luis Borges. No one who wants to understand the debate going on within the Catholic Church – or for that matter the main protestant churches – can fail to read the writings of Gustavo Gutiérrez, Jon Cortina or Leonardo Boff. There are, too, plastic artists from Latin America who are being recognised outside the region as great figures – Guillermo Roux, for instance, or Antonio Barrera, Wilfredo Lam or Orozco, Rivera and Siqueiros. No longer is the intellectual and artistic traffic between the two regions flowing only outwards from Europe.

Such ties as exist with Latin America do not exist between Europe and the Arab world, an area where fundamentalist forms of Islam are, for understandable reasons, rapidly gaining ground. The new Islamic fundamentalism, moreover, is only the most recent episode of a religious conflict which has kept the majority of Arabs and Europeans apart and at odds for more than 1200 years. As for India or Africa or the Far East, their cultural histories make those areas far less accessible than Latin America to a European.

Latin Americans, too, share with Europeans a political interest in not having their fate decided by the superpowers. Here the common feeling, it must be admitted, is muted by the differing experiences of each side. The Latin Americans have had more recent and personal bad experience of the Western superpower and have lacked the European experience of having to live beside a Soviet Union ruled by Stalin. The Europeans, who have seen the wars they brought on themselves resolved for the good by United States intervention, often cannot understand that anti-United States feeling in Latin America. They sometimes do not realise it has roots in simple national self-respect and is not the result of an obtuse commitment to dogmatic Marxism–Leninism. Over the Central American crisis Latin American governments have constantly found themselves on the same side as the Europeans in calling for an effective democracy and a peaceful, political settlement to issues. Both Latin Americans and Europeans have rejected the armed defence of the status quo which has often seemed to be the suggestion from the United States.

The twelve members of the European Economic Community and other European countries, notably Sweden, have committed themselves in a series of diplomatic pronouncements and protocols to aiding Latin American democrats. They have even sometimes lived up timidly to their verbal commitments by aiding genuine freedom fighters and distancing themselves from the dictators. Were they to do it more wholeheartedly it would benefit both Europeans and Latin Americans. The relationship, though often overlooked, is too valuable to be ignored.

# FURTHER READING

The most reliable and neutral economic information about the region comes from the United Nations Economic Commission for Latin America and the Caribbean, whose publications are available in Europe from United Nations Publications, Sales Section, Palais des Nations, 1211 Geneva 10, Switzerland.

The Inter-American Development Bank (808 17th Street NW, Washington DC 20577, USA) publishes an annual economic overview of the countries of the region – except Cuba – with extensive statistical appendices.

The publications of the Latin American Bureau (1 Amwell Street, London EC1R 1UL) provide a constantly updated source of information on the main social and economic topics of the region in the form of cheap booklets. The Catholic Institute for International Relations (22 Coleman Fields, London N1 7AF), which also runs the official and non-denominational British volunteer programme in several countries of Latin America, also publishes a continuous flow of excellent material on the region.

*The South American Handbook*, published annually by Trade and Travel Publications of Bath, is utterly indispensable for travellers to Mexico, Central and South America and the Caribbean.

Dr Leslie Bethell is editing *The Cambridge History of Latin America* (Cambridge University Press) in eight volumes, not all of which have yet been published. It is a superb work into which the non-specialist can dip with fascination on every topic from the Maya Indians to Spanish colonial mining methods and music.

In *The Land that lost its Heroes* (Bloomsbury, 1987), Jimmy Burns of *The Financial Times* tells the story of the Falklands War in the context of the rise and fall of the Argentine military dictatorship.

*The Lost Paradise* by Philip Caraman (Sidgwick and Jackson, 1975) is the classic history in English of the Jesuit Reductions in Paraguay.

Simon Collier's *From Cortés to Castro: An Introduction to the History of Latin America, 1492–1973* (Secker, 1974) is a general popular book, attractively written.

*Dictators Never Die* by Eduardo Crawley (Christopher Hurst, 1979) was written just before the Sandinistas overthrew the Somozas and is an excellent account of the life and times of that dynasty.

John Edwin Fagg's *Latin America: A General History* (Macmillan Publishing Co Inc., New York, and Collier Macmillan Publishers, London, 1977) is a good and exhaustive compendium of the region's history.

*Brazil: A Political Analysis* (Ernest Benn, 1979) by Peter Flynn is a thorough academic analysis of modern Brazil.

Richard Gillespie's *Soldiers of Peron: Argentina's Montoneros* (Oxford University Press, 1982) performs the difficult feat of explaining with gripping clarity the tortuous history of a particularly interesting urban guerrilla movement.

The Pelican Latin American Library, published in the early 1970s by Penguin Books and edited by Richard Gott, produced a number of political classics including Gott's own *Rural Guerrillas in Latin America*, Marcel Niedergang's *Twenty Latin Americas* and John Womack Jr's *Zapata and the Mexican Revolution*.

In *A State of Fear* (Eland Books, 1986), Andrew Graham-Yooll gives a chilling account of what it was like to be a journalist in the violent world of Buenos Aires in the 1970s.

John Hemming's *The Conquest of the Incas* (Harcourt Brace Jovanovich, 1973) is a very readable account of the way the Spaniards overcame the Andean empire.

A handy book on the Latin American novel has been edited by John King of Warwick University under the title *Modern Latin American Fiction: A Survey* (Faber and Faber, 1987).

John Lynch's *The Spanish American Revolutions, 1808–1826* (Weidenfeld, 1973) is, as everything else written by the former director of the London University Institute of Latin American Studies, elegant and authoritative.

Jenny Pearce's *Under the Eagle* (1981) and *Promised Land: Peasant Rebellion in Chalatenango, El Salvador* (1986) are respectively an account of US activity in the Caribbean Basin and a description of life in the zones under guerrilla control in that country published by the Latin American Bureau.

*Mexico: Inside the Volcano* (I. B. Tauris, 1987) has been a bestseller in the USA and in translation in Mexico itself. Written by Alan Riding, a distinguished British journalist now working for *The New York Times*, it is penetrating and frank and has upset many Mexicans and enthralled non-Mexicans.

*Peru 1890–1977: growth and policy in an open economy* (Macmillan, 1978), by Rosemary Thorp and Geoffrey Bertram, is the best modern economic study of that country.

# INDEX